# Exploring Data and Metrics of Value at the Intersection of Health Care and Transportation

## Proceedings of a Workshop



Theresa Wizemann and Alina Baciu, *Rapporteurs*

Board on Population Health and Public Health Practice

Health and Medicine Division

Transportation Research Board

*The National Academies of*
SCIENCES · ENGINEERING · MEDICINE

THE NATIONAL ACADEMIES PRESS
*Washington, DC*
**www.nap.edu**

**THE NATIONAL ACADEMIES PRESS 500 Fifth Street, NW Washington, DC 20001**

This project was supported by Contract No. DC-26-7392-00 between the National Academy of Sciences and the Federal Transit Administration, U.S. Department of Transportation. Any opinions, findings, conclusions, or recommendations expressed in this publication do not necessarily reflect the views of any organization or agency that provided support for the project.

International Standard Book Number-13: 978-0-309-44935-9
International Standard Book Number-10: 0-309-44935-9
Digital Object Identifier: 10.17226/23638

Additional copies of this publication are available for sale from the National Academies Press, 500 Fifth Street, NW, Keck 360, Washington, DC 20001; (800) 624-6242 or (202) 334-3313; http://www.nap.edu.



Printed in the United States of America

Suggested citation: National Academies of Sciences, Engineering, and Medicine. 2016. *Exploring Data and Metrics of Value at the Intersection of Health Care and Transportation: Proceedings of a Workshop*. Washington, DC: The National Academies Press. doi: 10.17226/23638.

*The National Academies of*
SCIENCES · ENGINEERING · MEDICINE

The **National Academy of Sciences** was established in 1863 by an Act of Congress, signed by President Lincoln, as a private, nongovernmental institution to advise the nation on issues related to science and technology. Members are elected by their peers for outstanding contributions to research. Dr. Marcia McNutt is president.

The **National Academy of Engineering** was established in 1964 under the charter of the National Academy of Sciences to bring the practices of engineering to advising the nation. Members are elected by their peers for extraordinary contributions to engineering. Dr. C. D. Mote, Jr., is president.

The **National Academy of Medicine** (formerly the Institute of Medicine) was established in 1970 under the charter of the National Academy of Sciences to advise the nation on medical and health issues. Members are elected by their peers for distinguished contributions to medicine and health. Dr. Victor J. Dzau is president.

The three Academies work together as the **National Academies of Sciences, Engineering, and Medicine** to provide independent, objective analysis and advice to the nation and conduct other activities to solve complex problems and inform public policy decisions. The National Academies also encourage education and research, recognize outstanding contributions to knowledge, and increase public understanding in matters of science, engineering, and medicine.

Learn more about the National Academies of Sciences, Engineering, and Medicine at **www.national-academies.org**.

*The National Academies of*
SCIENCES · ENGINEERING · MEDICINE

## PLANNING COMMITTEE FOR THE WORKSHOP ON EXPLORING DATA AND METRICS OF VALUE AT THE INTERSECTION OF HEALTH CARE AND TRANSPORTATION[1]

**YSELA LLORT** (*Chair*), Miami-Dade Transit (ret.), Miami, FL
**RICH GARRITY,** RLS & Associates, Inc., Dayton, OH
**PAUL HUGHES-CROMWICK,** Altarum Institute, Ann Arbor, MI
**JUDITH KELL,** Mercy Health, Muskegon, MI
**CATHERINE T. LAWSON,** State University of New York at Albany, Albany, NY
**PERRY MEADOWS,** Geisinger Health Plan, Danville, PA
**MICHELLE PROSER,** National Association of Community Health Centers, Washington, DC
**MARSHA REGENSTEIN,** George Washington University, Washington, DC
**ELAINE WELLS,** Ride Connection, Portland, OR
**NIGEL H. M. WILSON,** Massachusetts Institute of Technology, Cambridge, MA

*Staff*

**ALINA BACIU,** Project Director
**STEVE ANDRLE,** Project Director
**HOPE HARE,** Administrative Assistant
**CLAIRE RANDALL,** Program Officer

[1] The National Academies of Sciences, Engineering, and Medicine's planning committees are solely responsible for organizing the workshop, identifying topics, and choosing speakers. The responsibility for the published Proceedings of a Workshop rests with the workshop rapporteurs and the institution.

# Reviewers

This Proceedings of a Workshop has been reviewed in draft form by individuals chosen for their diverse perspectives and technical expertise. The purpose of this independent review is to provide candid and critical comments that will assist the institution in making its published Proceedings of a Workshop as sound as possible and to ensure that the Proceedings of a Workshop meets institutional standards for objectivity, evidence, and responsiveness to the study charge. The review comments and draft manuscript remain confidential to protect the integrity of the process. We wish to thank the following individuals for their review of this Proceedings of a Workshop:

**Barry Barker,** Transit Authority of River City
**Sharon Edgar,** Michigan Department of Transportation
**Commander Kent Forde,** Health Resources and Services Administration
**Ricardo Martinez,** Adeptus Health, Inc.

Although the reviewers listed above have provided many constructive comments and suggestions, they did not see the final draft of the Proceedings of a Workshop before its release. The review of this Proceedings of a Workshop was overseen by **Ned Calonge,** The Colorado Trust. He was responsible for making certain that an independent examination of this Proceedings of a Workshop was carried out in accordance with institutional procedures and that all review comments were carefully considered. Responsibility for the final content of this Proceedings of a Workshop rests entirely with the rapporteurs and the institution.

# Contents


ACRONYMS xi

1 INTRODUCTION 1
Organization of the Workshop and Proceedings, 4

2 TRANSPORTATION TO HEALTH-RELATED DESTINATIONS 5
FTA-Supported Transportation Efforts, 5
Environmental Scan of Other Transportation Efforts, 11
Discussion, 16

3 CROSS-SECTOR COLLABORATION TO PROVIDE TRANSPORTATION SERVICES IN URBAN SETTINGS 21
Telemedicine to Supplement In-Person Visits, 23
The Value of Relationships in Providing Services, 23
Transportation Planning to Improve Access to Primary Care, 25
Strategic Planning and Development, 27
Overview of the TRB Study *Between Public and Private Mobility*, 30
Discussion, 32

4 CROSS-SECTOR COLLABORATION TO PROVIDE TRANSPORTATION SERVICES IN RURAL/SMALL URBAN/SUBURBAN SETTINGS 37
Pathways to Better Health of the Lakeshore, 38

Protocol to Respond to and Assess Patient Assets, Risks, and Experiences, 41
HealthTran, 43
Children's Health Fund, 45
Discussion, 48

5 **REPORT BACK FROM BREAKOUT GROUPS** 53
Washington, DC, 53
Boston, Massachusetts, 56
Discussion, 57

6 **DATA SOURCES AND TOOLS FOR UNDERSTANDING AND ADDRESSING HEALTH-RELATED TRANSPORTATION NEEDS** 59
Community Commons, 60
Health Transportation Shortage Index, 63
National Health Interview Survey, 65
National Core Indicators-Aging and Disabilities, 66
Bureau of Transportation Statistics, 68
Discussion, 70

7 **CONNECTING PATIENTS TO TRANSPORTATION: INCENTIVES AND RETURN ON INVESTMENT** 75
Liberty, 76
Ride Connection, 79
Veterans Transportation Program, 81
Discussion, 83

8 **REFLECTIONS ON THE WORKSHOP** 89
Sponsor Perspective, 89
Participant Perspectives, 90

**APPENDIXES**
A REFERENCES 93
B WORKSHOP AGENDA 95
C ENVIRONMENTAL SCAN 101
D BIOSKETCHES OF SPEAKERS AND DISCUSSANTS 163
E STRUCTURED ANNOTATED BIBLIOGRAPHY* 189

* Appendix E is only available online at https://www.nap.edu/catalog/23638.

# Acronyms and Abbreviations

| | |
|---|---|
| ACA | Patient Protection and Affordable Care Act |
| ADA | Americans with Disabilities Act |
| APTA | American Public Transit Association |
| BTS | Bureau of Transportation Statistics (U.S. DOT) |
| CCAM | Coordinating Council on Access and Mobility |
| CDC | Centers for Disease Control and Prevention |
| CEO | chief executive officer |
| CHIP | Children's Health Insurance Program |
| CMS | Centers for Medicare & Medicaid Services |
| COPD | chronic obstructive pulmonary disease |
| CTAA | Community Transportation Association of America |
| DOT | U.S. Department of Transportation |
| ED | emergency department |
| EHR | electronic health record |
| EPA | U.S. Environmental Protection Agency |
| FAST | Fixing America's Surface Transportation Act |
| FHC | Family Health Center |
| FHWA | Federal Highway Administration (U.S. DOT) |
| FQHC | federally qualified health center |
| FTA | Federal Transit Administration (U.S. DOT) |

| | |
|---|---|
| GAO | Government Accountability Office |
| GIS | geographic information system |
| HHS | U.S. Department of Health and Human Services |
| HIPAA | Health Insurance Portability and Accountability Act |
| HMD | Health and Medicine Division (of the National Academies of Sciences, Engineering, and Medicine) |
| HRSA | Health Resources and Services Administration (HHS) |
| HUD | U.S. Department of Housing and Urban Development |
| n4a | National Association of Area Agencies on Aging |
| NACHC | National Association of Community Health Centers |
| NASUAD | National Association of States United for Aging and Disabilities |
| NCHS | National Center for Health Statistics (CDC) |
| NCI-AD | National Core Indicators-Aging and Disabilities |
| NEMT | nonemergency medical transportation |
| PRAPARE | Protocol for Responding to and Assessing Patients' Assets, Risks, and Experiences |
| RTAP | National Rural Transit Assistance Program (FTA) |
| TRB | Transportation Research Board (of the National Academies of Sciences, Engineering, and Medicine) |
| USDA | U.S. Department of Agriculture |
| VA | U.S. Department of Veterans Affairs |
| VHA | Veterans Health Administration (VA) |

# 1

# Introduction[1]

Two divisions of the National Academies of Sciences, Engineering, and Medicine, the Health and Medicine Division (HMD) and the Transportation Research Board (TRB), held a joint workshop on June 6–7, 2016, to explore partnerships, data, and measurement at the intersection of the health care and transportation sectors.

The workshop took place against the background of a promising policy context. The cost reimbursement structure for health care delivery has been shifting over time, in part due to the Patient Protection and Affordable Care Act (ACA), from a fee-for-service model to a value-based payments model. In the new context, providers have to work differently to achieve good outcomes and therefore assume a risk for readmission and other avoidable suboptimal outcomes. The ACA has also led to changes in tax-exempt hospital reporting, as it requires changes in the way hospitals deliver a benefit to the community commensurate to their tax exemption. In early 2016 the Centers for Medicaid & Medicare Services (CMS) issued a funding opportunity announcement for testing the "accountable health communities" model for linking clinical and community services. This model centers on testing three interventions that promote collaboration between clinical care and community services providers: (1) screening

[1] The planning committee's role was limited to planning the workshop, and this Proceedings of a Workshop has been prepared by the rapporteurs with the assistance of staff as a factual account of what occurred at the workshop. Statements, recommendations, and opinions expressed are those of individual presenters and participants and have not been endorsed or verified by the National Academies of Sciences, Engineering, and Medicine. They should not be construed as reflecting any group consensus.

community-dwelling Medicaid and Medicare beneficiaries for unmet health-related social needs (e.g., transportation); (2) linking beneficiaries to needed community services; and (3) encouraging alignment between clinical and community services to ensure that needed services are available to beneficiaries. The CMS announcement also refers to the agency's "better care, smarter spending, and healthier people" approach, which echoes the Triple Aim concept of better care and better population health at a lower cost, which has also played an important role in encouraging health care delivery systems to pay greater attention to population health and to tradeoffs in how the nation spends its health dollar. Finally, evidence from the public health sector demonstrates that health care is only one of the determinants of health, which also include genes, behavior, social factors, and the built environment (from sidewalks to transit). These contextual elements are key to understanding why health care organizations are motivated to focus beyond their walls and to consider and respond in unprecedented ways to the social needs of patients, including transportation needs.

The workshop began with a welcome from the executive directors of the two divisions, Clyde Behney (HMD) and Neil Pederson (TRB), who remarked on the importance of interdisciplinary collaboration, as exemplified by the workshop. In explaining the relationship between transportation and health care, Pederson said,

> Transportation does not exist to serve itself. Transportation really exists so that we can [try] to achieve other more important things in life and in society. Things like improving the economy, things like improving quality of life. And I think more and more we are starting to recognize that transportation has a role in terms of supporting public health as well.

Pederson situated the workshop in the context of a range of interactions that transportation has with health: safety, the spread of disease, environmental adverse health effects, healthy and safe transportation, access to health care services, and mobility for older adults and individuals with disabilities. Behney expressed an appreciation of the joint project's focus on data and measurement issues to help inform opportunities for the two fields to work together. He added that such a health sector concept as the learning health system and also lessons learned about trauma care in military situations could help improve transportation outcomes, too.

In her introductory comments, planning committee chair Ysela Llort said that the workshop was "taking place against a promising backdrop of policies, initiatives, and partnerships that are supporting greater attention to the social determinants of health at the population level and to the social needs of patients. Factors such as how individuals get to their doctor's appointment and to other essential destinations are increasingly part of decision maker considerations." She explained that workshop speakers and discussants would explore data, measurement, and value related to the issues of governance, industry, and research at the intersection of transportation and health care (see Box 1-1). Llort also emphasized that the workshop would not yield recommendations, although participants could make observations.

This intersectoral workshop was planned by a committee of 10 individuals, five with transportation sector expertise and five with health care delivery system knowledge. Chaired by Ysela Llort, the committee also included Rich Garrity, Paul Hughes-Cromwick, Judith Kell, Catherine Lawson, Perry Meadows, Michelle Proser, Marsha Regenstein, Elaine Wells, and Nigel Wilson. These 10 members outlined three objectives for the workshop and used them to guide the selection of speakers and the design of the sessions. The workshop was intended to (1) showcase models of transportation services that facilitate individuals' access to health care providers; (2) discuss data sources and information technology obstacles and solutions from and across the health care and transportation perspectives; and (3) explore opportunities to ascertain the value realized by transportation providers, health systems, and funders/payers—if providing transportation services results in improved health outcome.

**BOX 1-1**
**Statement of Task**

At the request of the Federal Transit Administration (FTA) of the U.S. Department of Transportation, the Health and Medicine Division and the Transportation Research Board will jointly convene an ad hoc committee to plan and conduct a 2-day workshop to examine data sources, including data from health care providers, existing measures, and other information relevant to using performance measures to explore the relationship between transit and health care (e.g., missed appointments) and to calculate the return on investment for public transit (including the Rides to Wellness initiative).

In preparation for the workshop, staff will commission individually authored papers to be presented and discussed at the workshop. A summary of the presentations and discussion at the workshop will be prepared by a designated rapporteur in accordance with institutional guidelines.

## ORGANIZATION OF THE WORKSHOP AND PROCEEDINGS

The first day of the workshop, which was titled Exploring Data and Metrics of Value at the Intersection of Health Care and Transportation, consisted of four context-setting presentations and a discussion (Chapter 2), followed by two panels on cross-sector collaboration to provide transportation services in urban (Chapter 3) and rural (Chapter 4) areas, and a breakout session with two concurrent sets of presentation and discussion to explore some issues in greater depth (Chapter 5). On the second day, the workshop continued with a panel that explored data and barriers (Chapter 6) and another panel that built on the data discussion by exploring the return on investment of and incentives to creating better cross-sector linkages to support patients (Chapter 7). The workshop concluded with a conversation in which individual speakers and participants discussed some of the ideas and themes they found meaningful, important, or actionable (Chapter 8). Workshop appendixes include Appendix D, an environmental scan prepared by Heidi Guenin to inform the workshop, and a structured annotated bibliography (Appendix E) intended to provide an overview of relevant peer-review and gray literature (reports, briefs, etc.).

In accordance with the policies of the National Academies of Sciences, Engineering, and Medicine, the workshop did not attempt to establish any conclusions or recommendations about needs and future directions, instead focusing solely on issues identified by the speakers, discussants, and workshop participants. In addition, the organizing committee's role was limited to planning the workshop. This Proceedings of a Workshop has been prepared by the workshop rapporteurs Theresa Wizemann and Alina Baciu as a factual synopsis of what occurred at the workshop.

# 2

# Transportation to Health-Related Destinations

To set the stage for discussion, Carolyn Flowers, the acting administrator of the Federal Transit Administration (FTA), provided a brief overview of FTA-supported efforts relating to transportation for accessing health care. Bruce Robinson, the acting associate administrator for program management at FTA, described the FTA Rides to Wellness initiative in more detail, and Oscar Gomez, the chief executive officer of Health Outreach Partners, discussed the Rides to Wellness Community Scan, a survey of the outcomes of missed appointments. Following the overview of FTA-supported efforts, Heidi Guenin, a senior associate at GridWorks, presented a synopsis of her findings from an environmental scan of health care and transportation partnerships around the nation, commissioned by the National Academies of Sciences, Engineering, and Medicine for this workshop.

The presentations were followed by comments from discussants Art Guzzetti, the vice president for policy at the American Public Transit Association (APTA); Heather MacLeod, the assistant director of physical infrastructure in the Seattle field office of the U.S. Government Accountability Office (GAO); and Judy Shanley, the vice president for education and youth transition at Easterseals, Inc. The session was moderated by Ysela Llort. (Highlights are presented in Box 2-1.)

## FTA-SUPPORTED TRANSPORTATION EFFORTS

The fact that some patients lack reliable transportation is a serious health care challenge, Flowers began. Although many warnings about health threats garner prominent media attention (e.g., the Zika virus, opi-

**BOX 2-1**
**Highlights and Main Points Made by Individual Speakers and Discussants[a]**

- Having health care coverage does not necessarily translate to access to care. The core barrier to accessing care is lack of transportation. (Flowers, Gomez, Robinson)
- There is also a need to help people at the individual level to understand the transportation options available to them and to help them through the process. Technology can offer promising approaches to help organizations and individuals navigate complex transportation systems. (Robinson, Shanley)
- Coordinated planning and partnerships are important. Governments and health care organizations vary widely across the country, and solutions will ultimately be local, responding to local concerns and carried out with local resources. Solutions that are developed locally can then be adapted and be applied across the country. (Flowers, Robinson)
- A key challenge is how to define and measure the success of investments in transportation and determine if improved access to health care improves health outcomes. To justify the need for transportation programs, data are needed about the impacts of missed appointments and the inability to get to care. (Flowers, Gomez, Pedersen, Robinson)
- The potential benefits of value derived from investing in transportation include reduced or avoided health care costs, social and personal benefits and avoided costs, and changes in health outcomes. (Guenin)
- The challenges and barriers to creating health and transportation partnerships include defining return on investment, funding, missing data, technology, geography, nonemergency medical transportation destination and service gaps, and cross-sector collaboration. (Guenin)
- The potential catalysts for health and transportation partnerships include grants, spaces for shared learning, start small and go slow, let patients tell the story, bring the care to the patients, customer service, sharing resources and increasing revenue, and sharing data and analyzing solutions. (Guenin, Shanley)

---

[a] This list is the rapporteurs' summary of the main points made by individual speakers and participants (noted in parentheses) and does not reflect any consensus among workshop participants or endorsement by the National Academies of Sciences, Engineering, and Medicine.

oid abuse, obesity), most people are generally unaware of the considerable impact that lack of transportation has on health. Overcoming this challenge, Flowers added, will require education and involvement of the public and leaders at the local, state, and national levels.

In 2008, 48.6 million Americans, or nearly 16 percent of the U.S.

population, lacked health care insurance, Flowers said. Today the uninsured rate has dropped to 9.2 percent, which is the lowest it has been in the past 50 years. Current enrollment in the health care marketplace is 12.7 million, she continued, and roughly 20 million people total are enrolled through the marketplaces, Medicaid expansion, young adults remaining on their parents' insurance, and other expanded coverage. The Patient Protection and Affordable Care Act (ACA) is built, in part, on the premise that regular, affordable access to primary care can lower costs and improve health outcomes over an individual's lifetime. However, every year approximately 3.6 million Americans miss or delay nonemergency medical treatment despite having health care coverage because they lack transportation to care (Myers, 2015). The ACA will be unable to live up to its full promise if people cannot get to care, Flowers said, and she shared some of the ways in which FTA is leading the search for solutions.

FTA has been working closely with the U.S. Department of Health and Human Services (HHS), the Centers for Medicare & Medicaid Services (CMS), the U.S. Department of Agriculture, the U.S. Department of Veterans Affairs (VA), and others to start the Rides to Wellness initiative (discussed further below). With the help of the Fixing America's Surface Transportation (FAST) Act,[1] Flowers said, FTA will be funding innovative programs to help connect people to health care through public transportation. The need is great, she said, and during the first round funding opportunity, FTA received proposals for more than three times the available funding. FTA is working quickly to identify and fund those proposals with the best chance for success. FTA is also holding regional forums across the country to bring together stakeholders in the transportation and health care industries who often rely on one another but who have had few chances in the past to consider these challenges together. In addition, FTA is fostering cooperation among federal agencies through the Coordinating Council on Access and Mobility (CCAM). The council was created in 2004 by executive order, and its work has been given new energy and focus through the FAST Act, which charges the council with publishing a strategic plan within the next year.

Because solutions will ultimately be local, responding to local concerns and being carried out with local resources, Flower said, it is very important that stakeholders come together (such as at this National Academies of Sciences, Engineering, and Medicine workshop) to consider the fundamental questions and share their results. In closing, she reiterated the point by Behney that one of the most important questions is how to define and measure the success of investments in transportation and how to understand

[1] More information on the FAST Act is available at http://www.fhwa.dot.gov/fastact (accessed August 4, 2016).

if improved access to health care facilities has made a difference in public health outcomes.

### Rides to Wellness Initiative

Transportation is a key factor in quality of life, Robinson said; it fosters healthy communities, promotes civil rights, and enables access to jobs, affordable housing, education, and training. As Flowers had explained, FTA launched the Rides to Wellness initiative to help address the important issue of transportation to health care. The initiative's goals are to leverage public transportation assets and services to improve access to health care, improve outcomes, and reduce health care costs, Robinson said. The vision is that through Rides to Wellness, people and community health will thrive. As FTA administered its grants to state and local providers, it saw an opportunity to leverage its investments together with other federal investments to help reduce the gap between health care and transportation. This initiative was supported by the FAST Act, which established a new FTA grant program with funding over 5 years for services related to nonemergency medical transportation (NEMT) and also established requirements related to CCAM (described by Flowers, above). Robinson said that this issue has been around for a very long time and that GAO has produced several reports for FTA with recommendations related to NEMT and to the coordination of rules and requirements across federal partners that provide transportation services. He also noted that years ago FTA had established the United We Ride program, an interagency initiative through CCAM, to help coordinate between transportation and human services programs.

In establishing the Rides to Wellness initiative, Robinson said, FTA was particularly interested in understanding challenges and solutions at the community level. One of the first programs launched was the Healthcare Access Challenge Grants program, which has provided grants to 16 communities to consider ways to improve access to health care and to bring new community partners into the discussion. Another approach, as had been mentioned by Flowers, is a series of regional forums where community grantees and members of the public transportation sector can engage on the issues and challenges facing communities. A recent regional forum in Charlotte, for example, included speakers from the Raleigh–Durham area who described the challenges of residents who may have insurance but who also have other barriers that make it difficult for them to understand how to access public transit or even how to get to health care when transportation is provided. Input from the regional forums indicates that the relevant issues are not only access to care and the availability of transportation, Robinson emphasized, but also the need to help individuals understand the options available to them and, in some cases, help them through the process.

The Rides to Wellness demonstration grant program has about $7 million available to fund promising projects and community solutions that are practicable. An important evaluation factor in reviewing programs, Robinson said, is how the partnerships among the transit agencies, health care organizations, and other nonprofit organizations are going to meet the transportation needs of stakeholders. Another important element of Rides to Wellness is the community scan project (described by Gomez, below). To be able to move forward and justify the need for these programs, he said, it will be important to collect data on the impact of missed appointments and the inability to get to care despite having insurance coverage.

Robinson shared several lessons learned thus far from the various discussions, regional forums, and initial grants process. A key lesson, he said, is the importance of coordinated planning and partnerships. He added that because both governments and health care organizations vary widely across the country, much of this work must be done at the community level. Challenges and solutions that are developed locally can then be adapted and be applied across the country. Another lesson is the need for people-first approaches, Robinson said. In many cases the solutions exist, but individuals do not necessarily know how to access those solutions; and technology offers promising approaches to help individuals navigate complex systems. One example could be for a person who is scheduling a health care appointment to also schedule his or her transportation at the same time, through some type of technology platform. Technology and research are central to helping develop the solutions for the challenge of transportation to health care, Robinson concluded.

### Rides to Wellness Community Scan by Health Outreach Partners

The mission of Health Outreach Partners is to build strong, effective, and sustainable health outreach models by partnering with local community-based organizations in order to improve the quality of life of low-income, vulnerable, and underserved populations (e.g., homeless, low-income seniors, farmworkers, immigrants). Health Outreach Partners supports outreach programs by providing training, consultation, and timely resources, Gomez explained, and it works to demonstrate the value proposition of prioritizing marginalized communities. The Rides to Wellness Community Scan project supports this approach, he said. Health outreach is a patient-centered approach to providing services that support health care but that are not reimbursable under the current system of care. Such services include, for example, health promotion, health education, facilitating access to care, coordinating care, fostering community awareness of underserved populations, and increasing the cultural competency of care providers. Measuring the impact or value of health outreach is challenging, Gomez said, because outreach programs are not transactional, but rather are based on building trust and relationships with individuals who have not previously accessed health care regularly, or at all.

Health Outreach Partners began to focus on transportation in 2011, with the Transportation Models that Work project, funded by The Kresge Foundation. Gomez said that in national needs assessments for health centers for the prior decade, transportation was always listed as the number one or number two barrier to care. That 3-year project identified and documented six successful case studies addressing transportation as a barrier to care; convened a National Policy Advisory Council, which produced a policy analysis and recommendations; launched a policy campaign to disseminate the findings; and incorporated lessons from the project into Health Outreach Partners' training and technical assistance activities.[2]

In 2016, Health Outreach Partners launched its transportation initiative, which consists of the Not Just a Ride project, funded by the Health Resources and Services Administration, and the Rides to Wellness Community Scan, funded by FTA.[3] Gomez reiterated the point made by others that for many individuals, gaining health care coverage under the ACA does not necessarily translate to having access to care. Certainly, relationship- and trust-building and overcoming fear of the system are key issues for first-time health system users, Gomez said, but at the core of the access issue is transportation. The Not Just a Ride project is designed to strengthen existing efforts at health centers. The project includes the development of transportation evaluation methodology for community health centers to assess the effectiveness and return on investment of their current transportation services for patients; cross-sector, peer-to-peer learning collaboratives to share case studies, strategies, and successes; and interactive online state transportation services and resource maps. Concurrently, the Rides to Wellness Community Scan will quantify the financial impacts of missed appointments. The first component of the project is a national survey of community health centers, VA medical centers, and private providers to identify the impact of the lack of transportation on health care costs. The second component is the development of profiles illustrating local communities that are adopting transportation solutions that show promising opportunities for return on investment.

[2] The full report for the Transportation Models that Work project, including the case studies, analyses, and recommendations, is available at http://outreach-partners.org/2014/06/04/overcoming-obstacles-to-health-care-transportation-models-that-work (accessed August 4, 2016).

[3] For more information, see http://outreach-partners.org/about-hop/transportation-initiative (accessed August 4, 2016).

Gomez closed with an anecdote from one of the case studies that emphasizes the challenges of capturing the value of transportation for health. In Hawaii, just outside of Honolulu, a community health center started a shuttle program that reaches seniors who live up on the mountainside and consequently have difficulty accessing care (Health Outreach Partners, 2014). The shuttle program, in partnership with other small businesses, stops at some of the senior homes to take residents to the health center, but the shuttle also stops at the pharmacy, a nutrition class, the grocery store, a Zumba exercise program, and other locations. Seniors are getting to their health care appointments and also meeting other personal and social needs that enhance health.

## ENVIRONMENTAL SCAN OF OTHER TRANSPORTATION EFFORTS

As background for the discussions, the planning committee for this National Academies of Sciences, Engineering, and Medicine workshop, with support from FTA, commissioned a scan of the landscape of health care and transportation partnerships, including the data being collected and shared, and how return on investment or value is being measured. The scan was conducted by Guenin, who presented a brief overview of her findings (the full report is provided in Appendix C). Approximately 70 people were interviewed for the environmental scan, including individuals working in health care, human services, and transportation services; researchers; consultants; representatives from foundations and other funders; and consumers and consumer advocates.

### Transportation Policies, Programs, and Services to Improve Access to Health Care and Health-Related Goods and Services

There are a variety of benefits of ensuring that individuals have transportation to health care and health-related services and destinations. Interviewees cited three types of benefits of investing in transportation in particular: reduced or avoided health care costs, social and personal benefits and avoided costs, and changes in health outcomes. Guenin developed a logic model for transportation access to health care in order to capture the relationships among resources, programs and policies, health factors, and outcomes (see Figure 2-1). She said that health factors can be a benefit in and of themselves in addition to leading to improved health outcomes, reduced health care costs, and other societal benefits. The challenge is how to define the return on investment and capture the relevant data for each of the interrelated elements relative to a given program's goals. Guenin said that biology and genetics are not included as health factors in her model

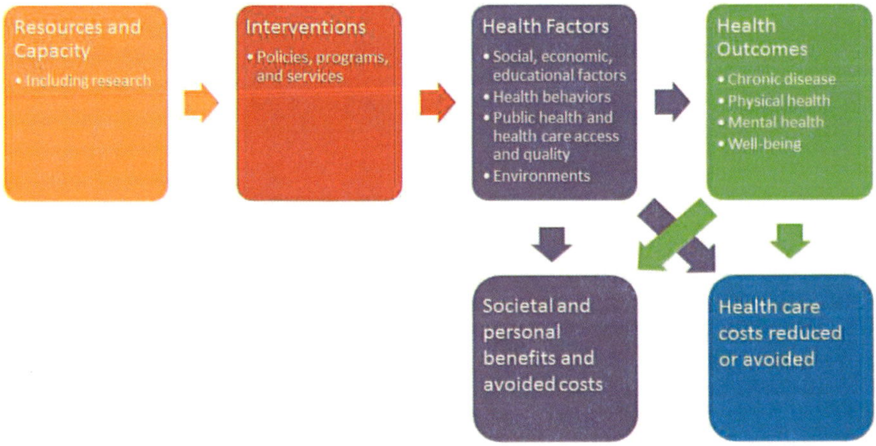


**FIGURE 2-1** Logic model for transportation access to health care.
SOURCES: Guenin presentation, June 6, 2016. See Appendix C. Based on models from County Health Rankings (http://www.countyhealthrankings.org/our-approach, accessed October 25, 2016) and NASEM, 2016.

because the model and the scan focus on the influence of programs and policies on outcomes.

Interviewees stressed that access to health care is not just about clinical care, and Guenin showed that, of the health factors listed, clinical care accounts for about 20 percent of the impact that policies and programs have on health outcomes. Social, economic, and educational factors have the largest impact, accounting for about 40 percent, with health behaviors accounting for another 30 percent, and environments for 10 percent (see Figure 2-2). In other words, clinical care is a relatively small part of what people consider to be very important when considering the investment made in transportation.

Based on the literature and the interviews, Guenin identified some of the main health outcomes that seem most affected by transportation access to health care (McClintock et al., 2016; Stiefel et al., 2016). For chronic disease these included asthma, cancer, cardiovascular disease, child oral health, child vision health, diabetes, disability, and obesity. For physical health the main outcomes affected by transportation access to care included exercise capacity, mobility, mortality, pain, sensory ability, and low birth weight. Outcomes related to mental health included depression, anxiety, and suicide. Overall well-being was also an outcome.

Guenin explained that the scan does not directly measure the impact of investments in transportation on health outcomes. Instead, proxy mea-

**FIGURE 2-2** Health care factors and proportion of impact on health outcomes.
SOURCES: Guenin presentation, June 6, 2016. See Appendix C. Revised from County Health Rankings model (http://www.countyhealthrankings.org/our-approach, accessed October 25, 2016) and 100 Million Healthier Lives Measurement System: Progress to Date (http://www.100mlives.org/measure/framework, accessed October 25, 2016).

sures are used, such as primary care utilization, emergency department utilization, missed appointments, transportation trips provided, and other data reflecting the provision of transportation and care. She said that interviewees were very interested in connecting the health and transportation datasets in order to better understand the impact of transportation on access to care and health outcomes.

With regard to transportation, Guenin said that there is a continuum of providers, modes of transportation, and entities that plan, design, and maintain the different transportation systems. Examples of these include public providers (e.g., fixed-route transit, fixed flexible route, demand responsive/Americans with Disabilities Act paratransit), commercial providers (e.g., wheelchair accessible, ambulatory with assistance, taxi-style service, stretcher service, ridesharing service), county-sponsored services (e.g., county-owned vehicles and drivers paid to transport Medicaid clients), first/last-mile connections (e.g., office/industrial park, neighborhood, military base, and university circulators), tribal transit, human services providers, veterans' affairs services, volunteer transportation, and personal transportation (with mileage reimbursement). Many of the transportation programs included in the scan are providers of NEMT for Medicaid clients accessing Medicaid-covered services. Other populations with which transportation providers worked included veterans, people experiencing multiple chronic conditions, pregnant women, children, individuals accessing drug treatment programs, older adults, people with disabilities, and rural residents.

## Themes from the Interviews[4]

*Barriers*

Interviewees were asked about the barriers and challenges they faced in creating health and transportation partnerships and in measuring the return on investment of transportation efforts. Guenin reported that responses fell into seven core theme areas:

1. **Defining return on investment.** Three main concerns were emphasized by interviewees: the value or return on investment outside of health care costs (returns may be nonfinancial, and actual costs may increase as more people access care or as currently unmet needs are met); the time-scale over which a return is being measured (e.g., some returns may be long term); and for whom a return is being measured (e.g., for insurers, patients, caregivers, the community).
2. **Funding.** Interviewees discussed the need to "go slow" and "start small" in the face of limited resources.
3. **Missing information and data.** Subthemes in this area included the need to ask the right questions (e.g., Why are patients missing appointments? How can one identify which patients are at risk for not having transportation options?); the impact of the ACA on access to insurance (which may result in increased costs in the short term); same-sector information gaps (i.e., not just between the transportation and health care sectors, but within each sector across providers, payers, services, etc.); and the impact of the Health Insurance Portability and Accountability Act (HIPAA)[5] on data sharing (leading to workarounds, e.g., embedding transportation staff in the health system, using non-health proxy data).
4. **Technology.** Recurring subthemes related to technology were the need for standardized data and open-source technology to support

[4] See Appendix C for more details.

[5] "The Health Insurance Portability and Accountability Act of 1996 (HIPAA) is a federal law that sets national standards for how health care plans, health care clearinghouses, and most health care providers protect the privacy of a patient's health information" (Source: CMS, at https://www.cms.gov/Outreach-and-Education/Medicare-Learning-Network-MLN/MLNProducts/downloads/SE0726FactSheet.pdf [accessed September 1, 2016]).

partnerships, client-side barriers to accessing available technology (e.g., a lack of awareness or understanding, technological limitations), and the difficulty of tracking trips on public transit.

5. **Geography.** Interviewees highlighted the transportation, health care, and measurement challenges that are specific to rural areas (e.g., an effective or efficient transportation system in a rural area may be different from that in an urban area, and different metrics are needed). Respondents also noted the barriers faced when crossing jurisdictional and service boundaries.
6. **NEMT destination and service gaps.** Interviewees emphasized issues specific to Medicaid, Medicare, and VA transportation, noting that some necessary destinations are not included (e.g., pharmacy, grocery store, support group) and that patients are unable to have caregivers or children ride along.
7. **Cross-sector collaboration.** The subthemes raised included issues concerning cross-sector knowledge (e.g., a lack of understanding of other sectors' language, operations, funding, programs, key contacts, etc.); different motivations and measures of success for different programs; coordination; and acknowledging that the implementation of solutions takes time (e.g., a too-rapid scale-up or trying to solve too many problems at once can lead to sustainability issues).

*Opportunities*

Interviewees also identified opportunities and potential solutions. Topics raised by individuals were organized by Guenin into eight main theme areas:

1. **Grants.** Interviewees emphasized the importance of grants in catalyzing partnerships.
2. **Spaces for shared learning.** Those interviewed highlighted the need for more opportunities and better ways to share knowledge and obtain guidance.
3. **Start small and go slow.** One of the most common themes, Guenin said, was that partnerships take time and resources to build. As mentioned above, interviewees emphasized the reasons for and benefits of starting small and going slowly, working within the available resources, and not attempting to solve too many issues at once.
4. **Let patients tell the story.** Interviewees noted the importance of listening to the end-users of services to understand their needs and

to determine if those needs are being met. The patient perspective also helps to make the case for funding and partnerships.

5. **Bring the care to the patients.** One transportation solution raised by several interviewees was the option of bringing the care to the patients (e.g., mobile care units, mobile pharmacy).
6. **Customer service.** Interviewees noted the value of providing good customer service and establishing relationships between service providers (i.e., drivers) and clients (i.e., patients).
7. **Sharing resources and increasing revenue.** Although some interviewees mentioned the challenges of cost sharing, Guenin said that some partnerships were able to find win–win solutions so that both the transportation and health care sides benefited.
8. **Sharing data and analyzing solutions.** Interviewees described various new tools and strategies for facilitating data sharing while maintaining compliance with HIPAA (e.g., cost allocation, proxies for health data, adding questions about transportation to community health needs assessments).

## DISCUSSION

Following the presentations, the panelists, discussants, and participants considered a variety of issues related to efforts to facilitate transportation to health-related destinations. Topics discussed included the lessons learned from recent mobility demonstration projects; transportation as a component of prevention; and the challenges of geography (e.g., the location of care, rural transit barriers), data availability, and funding gaps.

### Bridging Health Care and Transportation Issues

Over the past 6 or 7 years, at congressional request, GAO has conducted a series of studies looking at transportation-disadvantaged populations from the transportation perspective and has issued recommendations to FTA, MacLeod said. One study, for example, looked at the role of FTA in coordination, and another reviewed NEMT. Over the course of this work, GAO initially identified 80 federal programs that provide transportation services to transportation-disadvantaged populations and 42 federal programs that provide NEMT. MacLeod highlighted the challenge of obtaining data on programs, noting that, outside of FTA and a small number of other federal programs, federal agencies were unable to identify which of their programs provided these services or to provide any funding information. GAO was subsequently asked to review the transportation issues from a health care perspective and to make recommendations to HHS. This progression—and the workshop discussions thus far—illustrate the evolution of bringing the health care and transportation issues together, she said.

### Lessons Learned from Demonstration Projects

The National Center for Mobility Management is a national technical assistance center that disseminates information on mobility management and coordination and assists local communities in adopting proven transportation strategies to build community capacity, Shanley said. The center is supported though a cooperative agreement with FTA, and it operates in partnership with Easterseals, the Community Transportation Association of America, and APTA. The center has been involved in administering the FTA Rides to Wellness demonstration projects and providing technical assistance support to the grantees.

Shanley shared some of the lessons learned from the community demonstration projects, especially with regard to sustainability and replicability. Affirming the points made by Guenin, Shanley said that having the voices of riders at the planning table is critical. She mentioned a project funded by the HHS Administration for Community Living that is studying how to better engage people with disabilities and older adults in coordinated planning activities. Important elements of the demonstration projects included an educational component that helps patients navigate the transportation and transit services in the community; systemic data collection and evaluation processes built in during project design and development; multiple levels of data collection (e.g., individual/rider, organization/agency, and systems/community levels); technical assistance to support communities and partnerships; and peer-to-peer learning opportunities for grantees to share challenges and success. Shanley also noted the need for grantees to learn to use data to communicate and market their transportation solutions to the regional transition authorities and other stakeholders (e.g., potential funders and partners).

Shanley said that the lack of transportation to care has a ripple effect that is important to keep in mind. For example, transportation to care has implications for caregivers, Shanley said, and she added that the patient may also be a caregiver for a spouse or other family member. If that patient cannot regularly get to his or her chronic care appointments and ends up hospitalized, the family member for whom he or she cares might need to be placed in an institution.

### Prevention

Guzzetti raised the prevention aspect of transportation to health care and asked about any efforts to quantify the contribution of prevention to health outcomes. Guenin responded that current efforts measuring value and return on investment mostly consider primary care and the use of primary care versus emergency department visits and hospitalizations. At the county level, public health and medical health are having more collaborative conversations about their shared role in improving health, she said, and are starting to consider better ways to measure the impact of access and environments on such aspects as prevention. MacLeod added that prevention was considered briefly in a recent GAO study of NEMT service under the Medicaid expansion provision of the ACA. She reported that some states were applying to Medicaid for waivers so that they would not have to provide NEMT service for newly eligible populations. GAO was able to gather data on the states applying for or planning to apply for waivers and also on the reasons. In terms of the potential impacts, however, there was little information, and MacLeod expressed frustration at not being able to provide that information to congressional decision makers.

## Challenges

### *The Geography of Health Care*

Guzzetti said that health care has become consolidated and centralized over the past couple of decades. Neighborhood clinics, for example, are much less common, and people must travel farther to access care. Guenin said that in many cases primary care is still locally available, even in rural areas, but specialty services are often regional. She reiterated the added barrier of crossing jurisdictional boundaries for care. A patient seeking care at a regional facility may need to travel to the service border of one transit agency and then exit that transportation and wait for different transportation.

Martin Ornelas of the Rural Economic Assistance League, Inc., stressed the importance of developing rural models based on rural realities and not simply applying urban models to rural areas and assuming they will work. In addition to health professional and health facility shortage areas, rural areas have transportation shortage areas. Llort said that many medical centers are providing distance services through the Internet or other mechanisms. She acknowledged that many people have challenges engaging with technology, particularly the elderly, but she noted the need for more discussion on providing medical services in rural areas to individuals in their homes or other local bases.

Kate Lawson of the State University of New York at Albany raised the issue of coordination with partners in land use, and she asked whether anyone has been encouraging the health industry to consider developing facilities in empty shopping center spaces since they are most likely already on the transit system. Guenin replied that this was not raised by any of the interviewees.

*Data and Metrics*

Guzzetti called on the panelists to discuss what data and metrics are needed to advance the conversation and make progress on transportation and health care. MacLeod raised the topic of states using Medicaid transportation brokers to handle NEMT. About 5 years ago, she said, GAO asked states about coordination among their transportation programs and heard a lot of negativity around the Medicaid brokerages that were in place in some states. More recent surveys, however, show that some states are feeling more positive about the Medicaid brokerages and are even finding ways to coordinate and collect data through those brokerages. Unfortunately, she continued, GAO has been unable to determine how many states have brokerage systems or whether they are statewide brokerage systems or another model. Medicaid programs are state by state and can be complex, and even CMS does not have data on how many states have brokerages. Some of the brokerages are for-profit companies and could provide context concerning their riders and finances, she suggested.

*Funding Gaps*

Gomez said that funding for outreach and enabling services can be episodic or disease specific, making it very difficult to evaluate the program or demonstrate impact and value. Guenin agreed and added that interviewees reported that they would get funding and implement a program, and then the program would disappear when the funding ended. Patients who had become reliant on that program were left potentially in a worse situation. She mentioned that Oregon has a special transportation fund that is flexible, and this has helped to fill the gap when other funding for transit providers has ended.

# 3

# Cross-Sector Collaboration to Provide Transportation Services in Urban Settings

In urban areas, public transport traditionally plays a very significant role and is a very important part of the solution for bringing people to health care, said session moderator Nigel Wilson, a professor of civil and environmental engineering at the Massachusetts Institute of Technology. Public transport is not the entire solution, however, and panelists in this session shared examples of cross-sector collaboration to provide transportation services to health care in urban areas. Ann Lundy (via telephone), the vice president of Medicaid clinical operations in government programs at Health Care Service Corporation (HCSC), offered the perspective of a major health insurer, and described telemedicine as one solution to linking patients to care.[1] Perry Meadows, the medical director for government programs at Geisinger Health Plan, shared several real-life examples of where transportation and health care intersect. Yahaira Graxirena, a transportation planner at the Central Massachusetts Regional Planning Commission, and Xavier Arinez, the chief executive officer of the Worcester Family Health Center (FHC) discussed using geocoding to develop solutions and improve access to primary care for low-income and minority individuals. Mary Blumberg, the program manager for strategic planning and development at the Atlanta Regional Commission, described several examples from the Atlanta area of programs that increase patient knowledge about transportation options and strive to decrease unnecessary hospital readmissions. Finally, Katherine Kortum, a study director at the Transportation

[1] HCSC is the parent company of the Blue Cross and Blue Shield subsidiaries in Illinois, Montana, New Mexico, Oklahoma, and Texas.

Research Board (TRB) of the National Academies of Sciences, Engineering, and Medicine, provided an overview of the TRB study *Between Public and Private Mobility: Examining the Rise of Technology-Enabled Transportation Services.*

The presentations were followed by comments from discussants Jana Lynott, a senior strategic policy advisor for AARP; Barry Barker, the executive director of the Transit Authority of River City (TARC) in Louisville, Kentucky; Valerie Lefler, the president and chief executive officer of Liberty Mobility Now, Inc.; and Art Guzzetti. (Highlights are presented in Box 3-1.)

**BOX 3-1**
**Highlights and Main Points Made by Individual Speakers and Discussants**[a]

- By reducing the need for patient travel, telemedicine can enhance an existing relationship that a patient has with a health care provider, augment treatment and care plans already in place, and solve some of the transportation challenges. (Lundy)
- Relationships enhance the ability to provide quality service to patients (e.g., a relationship between a case manager and a health plan member or between a community health worker and a local transportation service provider). (Meadows)
- Transportation planning at the time of appointment scheduling can help to alleviate missed appointments, which are a significant source of financial loss for practices. (Arinez, Graxirena)
- Data sharing across sectors can be a barrier to collaboration. Tools are needed to allow sharing of patient information with the transportation authority, without compromising patient privacy. (Arinez, Graxirena)
- A lack of flexibility in program funding rules can inhibit pilot testing of innovative transportation solutions. In addition, many existing rules and requirements make it difficult to meet customers' needs (e.g., some transportation providers are prohibited from crossing county or state lines). (Barker, Blumberg, Kortum, Meadows)
- It is important to locate health care services in places where they can be accessed. Access to transportation and proximity of health facilities to transit stops should be taken into account when developing land. (Blumberg, Gomez, Guzzetti, Kortum)

[a] This list is the rapporteurs' summary of the main points made by individual speakers and participants (noted in parentheses) and does not reflect any consensus among workshop participants or endorsement by the National Academies of Sciences, Engineering, and Medicine.

## TELEMEDICINE TO SUPPLEMENT IN-PERSON VISITS

The Code of Federal Regulations requires states to ensure that eligible and qualified beneficiaries of Medicare and Medicaid have nonemergency medical transportation (NEMT) benefits, Lundy said. The transportation covered varies by state and is affected by such factors as geography and available modes of transportation. Providing NEMT can be particularly challenging in rural settings. This benefit does not cover transportation to other services that the patient might also need, such as community resources, food pantries, or counseling services, and Lundy suggested that there is room for improvement in this benefit. Depending on the beneficiary's needs and the state rules, NEMT services can be provided by taxi, personal car, public transportation, or other options. There are issues with each of those modes, Lundy said, especially around scheduling and the need for the beneficiary to be on time for certain treatments (e.g., dialysis, radiology services).

Lundy highlighted the ability of telemedicine to help address transportation to care issues. Some potential advantages of a telemedicine approach include reduced transportation costs, timeliness of appointments, efficient use of providers' time, increased access to specialty services or consultations, reduced numbers of emergency department (ED) visits for nonemergency care, a decreased risk of injury or disorientation for the beneficiaries (from not having to travel), and the ability to provide some preventive care and wellness screenings. With the implementation of electronic health records, a video visit could be stored in the patient's medical record, providing a real-time visual record of the visit. Telemedicine does not need to stand alone, Lundy stressed. Rather, it can enhance an existing relationship that the beneficiary has with a facility, local hospital, or clinic; augment care and treatment plans that are already in place; and solve some of the transportation challenges by reducing the need for travel.

## THE VALUE OF RELATIONSHIPS IN PROVIDING SERVICES

Meadows shared several examples from his experience at Geisinger Health Plan of cases where transportation and health care intersected. The first example involved a 65-year-old patient with chronic obstructive pulmonary disease (COPD) and debilitating pain. During her first 6 months of eligible coverage with Geisinger, the patient had 15 ED visits. She lived 15 blocks from her primary care provider's office but only two blocks from the ED, and because she did not have a car or money for transportation, it was easier to call emergency medical services and go to the ED. The patient also had 10 inpatient admissions related to the ED visits, and Meadows said that the cost of care for the ED visits and subsequent inpatient hospital admission was significant. Geisinger assigned a case manager to the patient, and although it took some time for the member to really trust the case manager, they were able to implement some solutions. The case manager arranged for taxi vouchers for the patient to be able to visit her primary care provider. During the following 5 months, the patient had only two ED visits, both resulting in inpatient stays related to her chronic kidney disease. The taxi vouchers have also allowed the patient to travel to her dialysis appointments and the pharmacy. Meadows said that although the cost of outpatient care for this member has increased (i.e., primary care visits, dialysis, medications), her inpatient costs were significantly reduced. Most importantly, Meadows said, the patient's quality of life has improved, and she is healthier and happier.

Another example is the Geisinger special needs unit, which is intended specifically for the Medicaid population. This model involves nurse case managers and social workers as well as community health workers who live in the area and can connect with the residents. One patient served by the special needs unit is a 42-year-old member with congestive heart failure, COPD, and diabetes who at one point weighed 600 pounds. This individual would require a bariatric ambulance to get to each of his doctor's appointments. A community health associate was able to arrange for all of this patient's providers to see him at one office in the hospital, during one day, over one 8-hour time period. The patient was transported by bariatric ambulance and was able to get all of the services he needed in one place. He has since had his bariatric surgery, has lost almost 300 pounds, and has improved health and quality of life. There was increased total cost based on the surgery, the inpatient stay, professional services, and pharmacy, Meadows said, but the end goal was improved health and quality of life.

The next example Meadows described was of a 3-month-old child diagnosed with retinoblastoma. This child needed transportation from Scranton, in northeast Pennsylvania, to a specialist in Philadelphia. The Medical Assistance Transportation Program in Pennsylvania will not cross county lines, and taking the shortest route to Philadelphia would require this patient to cross five county lines. This would have required this 3-month-old member and his mother to stand on a street corner, waiting for the next county service to pick them up, Meadows said (if they were picked up at all). A community health worker was able to use his local contacts to have a limousine service transport the child to the children's hospital in Philadelphia. Meadows added that this same community health worker just happened to be at a doctor's office when the para-ambulance that dropped a patient off could not be contacted to pick the patient up to take her home. The office was closing soon, so the community health worker used his contacts with one of the ambulance services to arrange transport for her at no charge.

The critical element in all of these example, Meadows said, is a relationship. Whether it is a relationship between a case manager and a health plan member or between a community health worker and local service providers, the relationship involves people working together to improve the health and quality of life of patients and plan members.

## TRANSPORTATION PLANNING TO IMPROVE ACCESS TO PRIMARY CARE

The Central Massachusetts Regional Planning Commission handles all of the planning for the Worcester Regional Transit Authority, Graxirena said. Through the National Center for Mobility Management design challenge and the Community Transportation Association of America (CTAA), the Worcester team was able to explore solutions for improving access to primary care for low-income and minority individuals who receive health care services at the Worcester FHC. The design challenge opened the door to collaboration, which was essential to understanding the patients' transportation needs and the magnitude of the problem, she said. She described the process and partners across four levels of collaboration: data collection to understand the magnitude of the problem, co-creation sessions to understand the patients' needs, discussions with peers for feedback and evaluation of solutions, and consideration of lessons learned from other models (see Figure 3-1).

The Worcester Regional Transit Authority registered more than 3 million passenger trips in 2015, Graxirena said. Twenty percent of all transit trips are for medical purposes, and the FHC is among the top 50 high boarding and alighting locations. Data collection for the design challenge began with a geocoding analysis done in association with the FHC. Graxirena and her Worcester FHC colleague Arinez both noted the challenges of sharing data across sectors and said that tools were developed to allow the sharing of patient information with the transportation authority without compromising patient privacy. For example, instead of seeking transportation data for the patient who lives at 200 Main Street, data would be collected for all the patients who are coming to the FHC from 0 to 500 Main Street, so individual patients could not be identified.

The geocoding analysis showed that even though the majority of FHC patients had access to nearby transit (living within 0.25 miles of a transit route), they needed to transfer through the main transit hub to reach the FHC. Some trips could take up to 3 hours. Overall, around 70 percent of FHC patients do not have a car and need some type of transportation arrangement (45 percent use the transit service, 15 percent share a ride, 10 percent use a livery service). Some patients said they cannot afford the bus fare. The FHC logs an average of 800 missed patient encounters per month,

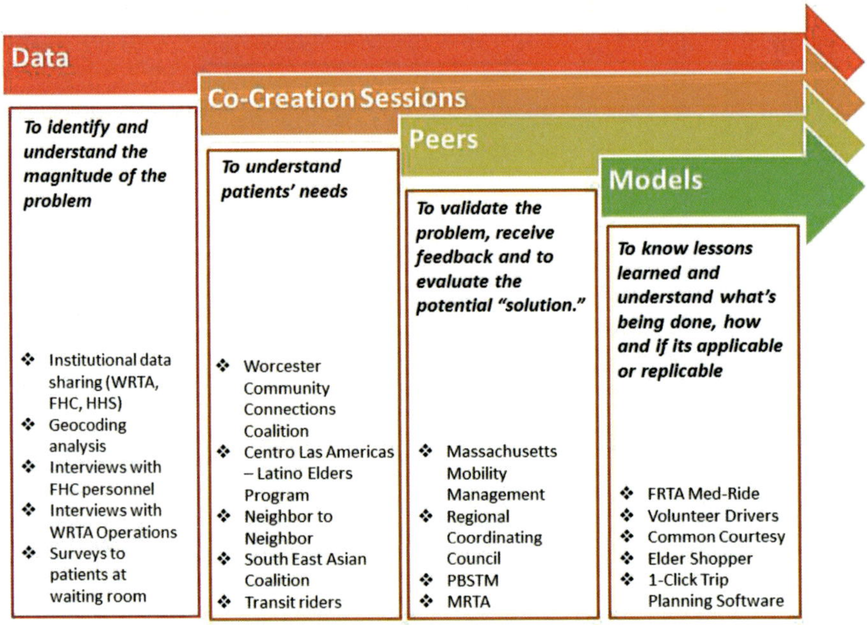


**FIGURE 3-1** Levels of collaboration.
NOTE: FHC = Family Health Center; FRTA = Franklin Regional Transit Authority; HHS = U.S. Department of Health and Human Services; MRTA = Montachusett Regional Transit Authority; PBSTN = Paratransit Brokerage Services, Transit Management, Inc.; WRTA = Worcester Regional Transit Authority.
SOURCE: Graxirena presentation, June 6, 2016.

at a financial loss for the FHC of nearly $1.5 million per year (at a rate of $154 per person per visit). The geocoding analysis found that 51 percent of patients had missed an appointment due to a transportation problem, which translates to a loss of nearly $740,000 for the FHC as a result of missed appointments due specifically to transportation problems.

Arinez said he was aware that transportation was an issue for many of his patients at the FHC, but he said he did not have the time or resources to do anything about it and was concerned that any attempts at change could take many years. Despite these reservations, the FHC embraced the design challenge project. One proposed solution was to integrate the scheduling of appointments with the bus schedule. The call center determines where patients are coming from and what routes they will take and schedules accordingly so the travel time for each patient is the shortest possible. Another solution is for the FHC to pay for a 1-day transit pass for patients at a cost of $3.50 each. It was calculated that 180 FHC patients daily use the Worcester Regional Transit Authority to get to the FHC. This would be a daily expense to the FHC of $630, or an annual expense of about $158,000 (based on 251 weekdays). This cost is only about 10 percent of the FHC annual loss due to missed appointments. Providing a transit stipend to patients who use it as their only means of transportation to access their primary care could lead to a significant savings for the FHC.

In closing, Arinez said that primary care systems are already at the limit and that there are not enough physicians in the United States to handle the increasing demand resulting from health care reform and increased coverage. In reducing missed appointments and increasing patient access to care, it will be important to also consider how to manage the increased burden on doctors and to avoid such problems as burnout and reduced quality of care.

## STRATEGIC PLANNING AND DEVELOPMENT

The Atlanta Regional Commission is both a metropolitan planning organization, which is responsible for transportation planning, and an area agency on aging, Blumberg said. She said that the transportation programs are supported through many different funding streams, each with different requirements, reporting, and unit definitions, making it challenging to compare data across programs. Blumberg shared several examples of transportation programs that the commission is working on.

### Bridge to Consumers

"You can have the best programs in the world, and if you don't have a bridge to the consumer, it really does very little good," Blumberg said. In particular, it is important that people know how to find the services. Through a grant from the FTA Veterans Transportation and Community Living Initiative, the Atlanta Regional Commission developed the Simply Get There trip discovery tool.[2] The tool, which is unique to the Atlanta region, pulls information from two different databases that are constantly updated, the area agency on aging service database (called ESP) and atlantatransit.org. The responsive design is meant for use with tablets, smartphones, and computers. Simply Get There covers specialized transportation, but at this time it does not have scheduling capabilities, Blumberg said. Travelers plan their trip in several easy steps: select the origin and destination of the trip; select specialized services if needed (e.g., wheelchair accessibility); select acceptable trip options (i.e., consumer chooses modes such as walk up to a half a mile, bus, train, vehicle for hire); and then

[2] See http://simplygetthere.org (accessed August 4, 2016).

review and select the travel plan based on personal factors (e.g., cost, time of arrival, length of travel). The project is now in phase 2 of development, and through an FTA Mobility Services for All Americans grant the application capabilities will be expanded to allow for trip transactions (e.g., centralized eligibility, booking, scheduling, dispatching, payment). The intent is to eventually release the design as open-source software so that others can use it, Blumberg said.

## FTA Section 5310 Program

Blumberg shared some data regarding the Atlanta Regional Commission's FTA Section 5310 program.[3] The Atlanta region has about 4.5 million people in 10 counties, but only three counties are covered by major train or bus systems, and many of the outlying counties have large gaps in transportation services. The Section 5310 program operates primarily through vouchers and serves 1,274 unduplicated riders per month. The majority are older than age 65 (82 percent), while 31 percent are persons with disabilities, and 17 percent are below the poverty level. The majority of trips (57 percent) are classified as personal, including quality-of-life trips (e.g., to the grocery, pharmacy, or senior center). About 39 percent of trips are for medical reasons, and 4 percent are for employment. From a cost perspective, the data indicate that the average Section 5310 program trip length is 12 miles one way, and the average cost to the system of that trip is $21. Blumberg added that mobility management costs are included in this cost-per-trip calculation, which is an important fact to know when comparing across regions as these costs are not always included. For comparison, she said, paratransit is $49.33 for a one-way trip, an average taxi ride costs $26.25, and Uber or Lyft can be anywhere from $15 to $20.

## Community-Based Care Transition Program

Another example described by Blumberg was a community-based care transition program aimed at reducing all-cause 30-day readmissions for Medicare fee-for-service patients by 20 percent across six hospital partners. This intervention, funded by the Centers for Medicare & Medicaid Services, had multiple components, including community health worker coaches who followed patients for 30 days post discharge, and assisted them with self-management skills. The area agency on aging also sought to

---

[3] For more information on FTA funding granted under Section 5310—Enhanced Mobility of Seniors and Individuals with Disabilities (49 U.S.C. 5310), see https://www.transit.dot.gov/funding/grants/enhanced-mobility-seniors-individuals-disabilities-section-5310 (accessed August 4, 2016).

address some of the social determinants of health, and enhanced services under the program included home-delivered meals, homemaker services, and transportation. Blumberg noted that these services were only for the 30-day post-discharge intervention.

Between October 1, 2014, and January 31, 2016, the program served 8,400 people. Only 6 percent (464 people) were enrolled in and receiving transportation services. The baseline readmission rate was 19.4 percent. The standard intervention reduced readmissions to 15 percent, and for those receiving transportation services readmission was reduced to 7 percent. It is not possible to attribute this further reduction specifically to transportation, Blumberg cautioned, as other services (e.g., meals) might have contributed, but it is a very interesting observation. Total Medicare cost savings from the reduced readmissions for the cohort without transportation services (n = 7,937) was calculated to be $236,544, while the total savings for those receiving transportation services was nearly $400,000, even though it was a much smaller number of people (n = 464). Those receiving transportation services were also 7 percent more likely to make it to their follow-up appointment within 14 days of discharge.

## Opportunities

Blumberg shared her perspective on some of the challenges and opportunities for implementing transportation services. More funding flexibility at the local level would allow for more innovation, she said. For example, the Section 5310 funding program goes though the state agency, and there are layers of rules, mainly designed for traditional transportation fleets, that are imposed on Atlanta's Section 5310 programs (e.g., required training in cardiopulmonary resuscitation) that add burdens to testing innovations. Although Uber or Lyft may have some safeguards, insurance, and training for drivers, they do not have health-related training, and this is a barrier when attempting to pilot innovative approaches with such services. Another area where flexibility is needed is transportation for dialysis patients. Dialysis centers benefit greatly from patients having reliable transportation, yet federal rules prohibit the Atlanta Regional Commission from approaching patients to be reimbursed for transportation services.

Blumberg also highlighted the importance of designing programs at the outset to address predefined research questions and capture the necessary data. She recommend testing a multi-funding data pilot in which several programs would agree to some common research questions and collect uniform data across all the multiple data sources of the programs.

Another opportunity is improving provider capacity through training and education combined with implementing technology to efficiently deliver services and capture data. Some rural areas are still capturing data with pen and paper, Blumberg said. Travel training is also needed, not only for consumers, but also for health care providers, social workers, and caseworkers, Blumberg said.

Moving forward, the Atlanta Regional Commission will continue to test and improve data collection to measure program outcomes and drive system improvements, she said. The ultimate goal, Blumberg said, is to maximize transportation dollars by matching consumers' desires and abilities to the right level of service for them.

## OVERVIEW OF THE TRB STUDY *BETWEEN PUBLIC AND PRIVATE MOBILITY*

In December 2015, TRB released its findings from an 18-month study of shared mobility services in Special Report 319, *Between Public and Private Mobility: Examining the Rise of Technology-Enabled Transportation Services* (TRB, 2016). The report considered a wide range of policy issues surrounding different mobility services, and Kortum provided a brief overview of the findings most relevant to the issue of health care access.

There are many innovative mobility options and services that are changing the way that people get around. Some example are car sharing, bike sharing, taxis, transportation network companies (e.g., Uber, Lyft), and microtransit services.[4] Most of these mobility services are based around smartphone applications, and the report discusses the equity concerns associated with the growing dependence on smartphones for these services. Smartphones tend to be fairly prevalent across a wide range of income spectrums, Kortum said, but there is an age divide that exists with smartphones and other technology that is causing accessibility concerns.

There are also both accessibility benefits and drawbacks of smartphone-application-based mobility services for people with disabilities. Blind persons, for example, have long had difficulty hailing a taxi on the street, and an app-based service can help to overcome this. There are advantages to making a digital payment through smartphone mobility applications. For example, there is no question about what money the person is handing over or what change was received. Kortum noted that there have been some issues regarding service animals, including animals being placed in the vehicle trunk, or drivers denying the passenger the ride. Because Uber and Lyft drivers are independent contractors and not employees, those trans-

---

[4] As defined in the report, *microtransit* "encompasses flexible private transit services that use small buses (relative to traditional transit vehicles) and develop routes based on customer input and demand" (TRB, 2016, p. 17). Examples of microtransit service companies [at the time of report publication] include Bridj, Loup, and Chariot.

portation network companies have a limited amount of control over driver behavior and availability, but they are working to address these issues.

Another potential barrier to accessing mobility services that are based on smartphone applications is the need for a bank account or credit card for payment, since some estimates suggest that 20 percent of the U.S. population have neither bank accounts nor credit cards. There is a lot of overlap between the vulnerable populations that need these transportation services and those who do not have smartphones or bank accounts.

Kortum suggested that taxis are currently somewhat better suited for handling health-related trips, in part because taxi drivers tend to have more experience with helping people who need assistance in and out of a vehicle. There is also a long history of cooperation between paratransit agencies and the taxi industry. Kortum said that people in wheelchairs are only a small subset of the paratransit population. Many people in need of paratransit can ride in regular vehicles, but they just do not have easy access to them (e.g., transit routes are not near enough, transit stops are not accessible). Paratransit agencies often partner with local taxi companies to provide rides for these individuals. Transportation network companies are very interested in getting into this market, Kortum said. An advantage of paratransit partnering with Uber or Lyft is that these services are not subject to the same jurisdictional restrictions that much of the taxi industry often is. Shared mobility services are working toward improving access, including allowing people to call into a central dispatch system (eliminating the need for a smartphone application), allowing riders to specifically request a wheelchair-accessible vehicle, and having drivers who are trained to help people in and out of a vehicle.

In some places, low-income individuals (e.g., those on welfare or receiving food stamps) are eligible to receive reduced-cost bikeshare passes, Kortum said. The Boston Medical Center has launched a program called Prescribe-a-Bike, in which doctors can prescribe a free bikeshare membership for their low-income patients, which provides both a means of transportation and a healthful activity. The city of Birmingham, Alabama, has partnered with Blue Cross to provide "pedelecs," electric pedal-assist bicycles that make it easier to participate in shared mobility throughout the year. One public health issue that has come up regarding bikeshare, Kortum said, is whether helmets should be required and whether that would deter people from using the bikeshare.

The TRB study also reviews the wide range of policy and planning issues surrounding shared mobility.

## DISCUSSION

Following the presentations, panelists, discussants, and participants discussed a variety of issues, including the data resources available to participants and some issues related to data collection; collaboration and partnerships; the challenges of existing rules and regulations; and the location of health services relative to the users of those services.

### Data Collection and Resources

Lynott apprised participants of the AARP Public Policy Institute's new Livability Index,[5] which uses data from more than 50 different sources to score the overall livability of neighborhoods and communities, as well as providing scores in seven categories (housing, neighborhood, transportation, environment, health, engagement, and opportunity). Transportation-related data include such factors as speed limits, transportation-related injuries and fatalities by neighborhood, the environmental footprint and adverse health effects of transportation, near-roadway pollution, healthy and safe transportation options, the availability of public transportation services, state support for volunteer driver programs, coordinated human services transportation, and enhanced mobility for older adults and people with disabilities. There are also data on neighborhood characteristics that support health, such as walking trips per household per day, the general walkability of the neighborhood environment, and proximity of grocery stores. The next phase of research, Lynott said, will be to combine the livability data with other major federal datasets and health datasets to study how those community characteristics affect health.

Lynott also mentioned the National Household Travel Survey, which reviewed travel trends from 1969 through 2009. From 1983 through 2009, trips for medical purposes increased 187 percent, she said. This increase was consistent across all age groups (i.e., it was not due to population aging) and was likely related to major changes in the health care sector and in how people access health care, which led to greater demand. All Americans have to travel more to access health care than they have in the past, she said.

With regard to data collection for assessing value, Lynott suggested that there is a need not only to consider fixed route public transportation, but also to demand responsive transportation. Data should show not only whether there is transit service to a particular county, but also the true availability of the service (e.g., hours of the day and days of the week that

[5] Graphics, metrics, and other resources available at https://livabilityindex.aarp.org (accessed August 4, 2016).

service is available). She also noted the need for transit providers to upload their data to the Google Transit Feed Specification (GTFS).[6] The AARP Livability Index used GTFS data, so if a state has not uploaded its data, even though it may have transit in every county, it is getting scored very low on those indicators.

### Community Collaboration

Lynott asked the panel whom the transportation community should reach out to in the health care community to start a collaboration in their area. Meadows said that in a large health plan, such as Geisinger Health Plan, it would be someone like himself (e.g., the medical director for government programs). Specifically, he recommended approaching the health care side first (e.g., the head of case management, the chief medical officer) and let people on that side take it to the finance department. If they can show a health care benefit, they can get buy-in from the finance side. Arinez agreed and added that it takes some effort from health care organizations to think about the entire visit cycle, from the time a patient leaves home to the time he or she returns. An hour-long office appointment could be a 6-hour event for the patient. Graxirena said that the Worcester Division of Public Health, through the Community Health Improvement Plan, is leading the conversation between the transit agency and the health care facilities, health care providers, and other community organizations. Gomez said that hospitals now have standardized community benefit requirements,[7] and he suggested approaching hospitals to consider transportation as part of their community benefit efforts.

Lefler asked if there were any examples of how an urban and a rural transit system partnered to improve access to care or provide last-mile assistance. Graxirena said that in Worcester the transit authority has agreements with other transportation providers outside the fixed route. This allows for the transportation of people to their jobs, medical appointments, or other areas that are outside the paratransit service boundary.

---

[6] GTFS "defines a common format for public transportation schedules and associated geographic information. GTFS 'feeds' let public transit agencies publish their transit data and developers write applications that consume that data in an interoperable way" (https://developers.google.com/transit/gtfs [accessed August 9, 2016]).

[7] Such requirements were imposed on tax-exempt hospitals and health systems by the Patient Protection and Affordable Care Act under the Internal Revenue Code, and they standardize "what counts as a community benefit" and require "specific information about [hospital] policies and practices relating to community health needs assessment, financial assistance, hospital charges, billing and collections, and the other new federal requirements for charitable hospitals" (http://www.hilltopinstitute.org/publications/WhatAreHCBsTwoPager-February2013.pdf [accessed August 8, 2016]).

Barker reiterated the comments by panelists about the value of relationships and of embedding people in partner organizations. Each organization has different languages, motivations, and reward systems. Referring to the transportation authorities and their ability to tackle systemic issues, including access to health care services, Barker also urged health sector colleagues to "come to us with what you need. Let us figure it from there, because there's some very creative ways to do it."

### Rules, Regulations, and Safety

Barker expressed concern about being so laden with rules and requirements that it is difficult to meet customers' needs or implement solutions. In addition, customers should not have to become experts in transportation regulations to be able to use the services. Barker suggested that there is a need for more ombudsmen who can help people navigate the system on a one-to-one basis.

Kortum underscored the need for creating flexible, guiding regulatory policies that are in everybody's best interest, as opposed to those that are largely mirroring the status quo for the transportation industries that already exist (e.g., taxis). There are ways, through regulations and policy, to create more partnerships. Some cities are moving in this direction, she said.

A participant raised the issue of safety when sending patients via transportation network companies. He noted that Uber and Lyft recently suspended operations in Austin, Texas, because of a regulation requiring improved background checks (including fingerprinting). He highlighted the need for transportation network companies to work with the health care sector to reduce the risk of lawsuits in contracting patient transport services to Uber or Lyft. Kortum pointed out that the taxi industry is required to fingerprint drivers, and the practice is common in a variety of professions that have a public safety aspect (e.g., school employees). Uber and Lyft require background checks conducted through background check providers, which include driving history and criminal background checks based on name and birthdate. Kortum added that there has been no analysis regarding which approach provides a more complete background check (fingerprints versus name, birthdate, and Social Security number). Fingerprinting is considered standard practice, but there are time and financial costs associated with fingerprinting, and the benefits over other background check methods are not clear.

### Land Use and Location of Health Services

Guzzetti raised the issue of land use and the need to locate health care services in places where they can be accessed. Blumberg said that in light of changing demographics (people living longer and a growing cohort of older people), it is even more critical that transportation, housing, and health care all be connected. Developers have been branding it as new urbanism, and consumers are demanding more walkable, livable communities. Gomez highlighted the value of locating community health centers near transit stops. He said that this does not necessarily occur to developers, and he encouraged participants to discuss this with their community health centers as they are building new access points. Guzzetti observed that connecting transit to airports has become a focus for many cities because it draws conventions and tourism. Some cities have started to do this for health as well. Cleveland, for example, has a bus rapid transit line—the Healthline—that connects to city health facilities. He wondered how the "branding" of transit and health linkages could be enhanced, as has been done for airports linked to cities.

Kortum observed that some cities are looking at shared mobility in lieu of parking. In San Francisco, for example, some developments are providing vouchers for transit in lieu of parking for residents who do not bring a car. Car sharing and bike sharing are also becoming popular amenities for new developments, specifically in urban centers, and some new residential developments are providing dedicated car-sharing spaces in their parking garages.

Arinez said that the Worcester FHC is collocating services in one building, including dental, radiology, vision, behavioral health, and pharmacy services. An outcome of this that insurance companies should be aware of is that when the patient cannot make it to the office, he or she is missing six appointments, not one, and it is a significant financial loss.

# 4

# Cross-Sector Collaboration to Provide Transportation Services in Rural/Small Urban/Suburban Settings

When transporting people and goods, there are often first-mile, last-mile issues to be addressed (i.e., how does the person get from home to transit, and then from transit to the final destination). In rural settings these become "first 50 mile, last 50 mile issues," said moderator Rich Garrity, a senior associate at RLS and Associates. Speakers in this session continued the dialogue on cross-sector collaboration, but with a focus on suburban, small urban, and rural areas. Judy Kell, the hub operations manager for Pathways to Better Health of the Lakeshore, in Michigan, discussed efforts to link residents to the social determinants of health as well as the need for coordination across health, social services, and transportation. David Faldmo, the medical director and quality director at the Siouxland Community Health Center in Sioux City, Iowa, described the Protocol for Responding to and Assessing Patients' Assets, Risks, and Experiences (PRAPARE) assessment tool that providers can use to screen for and address the social determinants of health, including transportation. Suzanne Alewine, the executive director of the Missouri Rural Health Association and co-founder of Community Asset Builders, described HealthTran, Missouri's Rides to Wellness initiative. Dennis Johnson, the executive vice president for policy and advocacy and government affairs at the Children's Health Fund, described using mobile health clinics to bring care to children in underserved communities.

The presentations were followed by comments from discussants Charles Carr, the director of the Office of Intermodal Planning for the Mississippi Department of Transportation; Amy Conrick, an assistant director for the Community Transportation Association of America (CTAA); Robin Phillips, the executive director of the National Rural Technical Systems

**BOX 4-1**
**Highlights and Main Points Made by Individual Speakers and Participants[a]**

- Kell, representing a health system, and Faldmo, representing a community health center, both emphasized the need to screen for and address the social determinants of health (or, as Kell put it, the social determinants of care), including access to transportation, and also emphasized the need for care coordination across health care and social services silos (e.g., scheduling the appointment and arranging for transportation at the same time). (Faldmo, Kell)
- Using data to demonstrate the financial value of transportation to health care is the way to achieve policy change (e.g., data demonstrating the significant financial losses due to missed appointments). (Alewine, Johnson)
- Children are especially at risk for missing health care appointments due to the unavailability of transportation during open clinic hours (e.g., the parent is at work with the car). This can mean missed immunizations and routine well-child care; an increased incidence of untreated chronic illnesses (e.g., asthma); an increased use of emergency departments for nonemergency care; and an increase in preventable hospitalizations. (Johnson)
- Funding is an issue of significant concern in rural areas (e.g., state funding for rural transportation is very limited; many rural areas rely on FTA rural funding programs; FTA Section 5311 program funding is limited; programs have experienced delays in receiving Section 5310 dollars; the procurement process is cumbersome; health care organizations do not understand the way that rural transit is financed). (Alewine, Phillips, Stock)

[a] This list is the rapporteurs' summary of the main points made by individual speakers and participants (noted in parentheses) and does not reflect any consensus among workshop participants or endorsement by the National Academies of Sciences, Engineering, and Medicine.

Program; and Marianne Stock, division the chief of Rural and Targeted Programs at the Federal Transit Administration (FTA) of the U.S. Department of Transportation. (Highlights are presented in Box 4-1.)

## PATHWAYS TO BETTER HEALTH OF THE LAKESHORE

Muskegon County, Michigan, has a population of 172,000 and includes three very urban areas that are entitlement communities as well as suburban areas and rural areas that are large farming areas, Kell said. The county has 28 governmental units and 14 school districts. Twenty percent of the children in the county live in poverty, and only 58 percent of the adult population has attended some college. The county ranks 81st of 83 Michigan counties in health risk behaviors and is below state and national standards for low-birth-weight babies.

People live in environments that do not support them, Kell said, and the Pathways to Better Health of the Lakeshore program links the people of Muskegon to the social determinants of care: housing, transportation, food, utility assistance, and anything else that might improve their health status. Community health needs assessments[1] indicated that care coordination was desperately needed, not just among doctors, nurses, and specialty clinics, but across health and social service silos, including transportation, which Kell said was the main barrier for the population. Pathways to Better Health of the Lakeshore is administered by the Health Project, which is the community benefit ministry of the Mercy Health System. The program relies on community health workers who are indigenous to the community in which they work. The community health workers assist people in navigating the health care system, including linking them to transportation and assisting them en route as needed. The community hub coordinates all of the health care and social determinants of care for people in the program and provides clinical oversight to those community health workers who are deployed to assist. The budget for the hub includes funding for transportation, Kell noted. Any provider (e.g., hospital, emergency department [ED], clinic, physician office, etc.) can refer a patient into the hub. Patients are then referred out to the community health workers. The Pathways program uses an electronic record with checklists that assess eligibility and identify access to care, financial issues, and health improvement barriers. Pathways programs include, for example, medical home, medical referral, health coverage, social service, transportation, pregnancy, and smoking cessation. The program works through the barriers, provides documentation that the patient received the services needed, and creates accountability for the patient, agency, and health system. Community partnerships also play a role. Kell said that Muskegon was designated by the U.S. Environmental Protection Agency as a sustainable community and was provided with a transportation consultant who engaged all 28 governmental units and others in the community to develop a transportation plan. The plan included mobility coordinators and cross-sector collaboration among Muskegon County public transportation; private cabs; 10 care coordinating agencies that work with Mercy Health's community health workers (including

---

[1] Kell reminded participants that nonprofit hospitals must conduct a community needs assessment as part of their filings with the Internal Revenue Service in order to maintain their nonprofit tax status. Hospitals are then required to develop an implementation strategy with goals, objectives, and measurable outcomes for their efforts to improve health status in the communities.

federally qualified health centers, the Area Agency on Aging, the health departments, and a variety of social service agencies); churches, libraries, and public housing (which provide space for the community health workers to hold workshops on chronic disease management); and informal relationships with rural county transportation services. In addition, three buses were funded by the U.S. Department of Transportation (DOT) to extend routes out to three rural areas.

Initial evaluation results show that spending was lower than the comparison group prior to and after the Pathways program, and the data suggested that patients were receiving better care. Kell shared several examples of the impact of connecting patients to transportation. Patients in the Healthy Pregnancy Program, for example, reduced their number of ambulance rides to the ED by 25 percent. They now take cabs or the bus to a care provider. Patients in all Pathways programs are provided transportation to their Alcoholics Anonymous and Narcotics Anonymous meetings, along with treatment. There was also a $2.4 million cost reduction for the hospital system as a result of decreased use of the ED and increased use of nonemergency transportation and primary care visits. Participation in the workshops also decreased social isolation for patients.

Kell identified several barriers to implementing the Pathways program including, as was mentioned by other speakers, crossing county or state lines to access services. In addition, the definition of disability is confusing to some partners when determining eligibility for programs. In general, there is a lack of data to justify the investment in transportation for health care. There were also contract issues and stakeholder confusion or inertia.

In moving forward with cross-sector collaboration to provide transportation, Kell suggested the following steps:

- Find a champion and develop partnerships.
- Inform the community.
- Engage the patients as advocates for system change.
- Participate in local community needs assessments.
- Develop strategies and implement them via pilot projects.
- Develop data and return-on-investment studies.
- Seek change on the state and federal levels related to boundaries, funding, and definitions of disability.
- Institutionalize partnerships and funding.

In the case of the Pathways program, for example, the champion is the community. The program has been institutionalized through the use of community benefit dollars through the health system, and community members are encouraged to participate in their local community needs assessments.

## PROTOCOL TO RESPOND TO AND ASSESS PATIENT ASSETS, RISKS, AND EXPERIENCES

Faldmo described the PRAPARE assessment tool as an example of a program that is addressing transportation needs. According to the National Association of Community Health Centers' website, PRAPARE's funding came from The Kresge Foundation, the Blue Shield of California Foundation, and the Kaiser Permanente National Community Benefit Fund at the Easy Bay Community Foundation.[2] The protocol's main objective is to create a tool that community health centers and other health care providers can use to screen for and address the social determinants of health, including transportation. PRAPARE also is intended to inform the development of community partnerships, to develop new programs to help overcome the social barriers to good health, and to decrease health care spending.

The Siouxland Community Health Center is part of a team of five states where community health centers are using the same electronic health record (EHR) system, Faldmo explained. Part of the project is to screen for social determinants of health and record them in the EHR. PRAPARE was designed specifically to aid health centers in gathering data that inform and address individual patient care and population health management, while capturing what makes health center populations unique. However, there are also local-, state-, and national-level goals, including informing advocacy efforts related to local policies concerning the social determinants of health (see Figure 4-1).

In using PRAPARE, patients are asked about transportation as well as whether lack of transportation has kept them from a medical appointment or from getting their medications. Faldmo shared data showing that 17 percent of patients being served by the six centers in Team 4 had transportation needs. That is nearly one out of every five patients who had a transportation need that kept them from getting the health care they needed, Faldmo emphasized.

### Siouxland Community Health Center

Sioux City, Iowa, has a population of about 85,000 people, but becomes very rural, very quickly just outside of the city, Faldmo explained. Many of the Siouxland Community Health Center patients come from the outlying rural areas, and, as the city is in a tristate area, many of the patients come from South Dakota and Nebraska as well. The center has medical care (including urgent care, HIV care, and some behavioral health care), dental care, and a pharmacy all in house. There are about 95,000 patient visits per

---

[2] See http://nachc.org/research-and-data/prapare (accessed September 22, 2016).

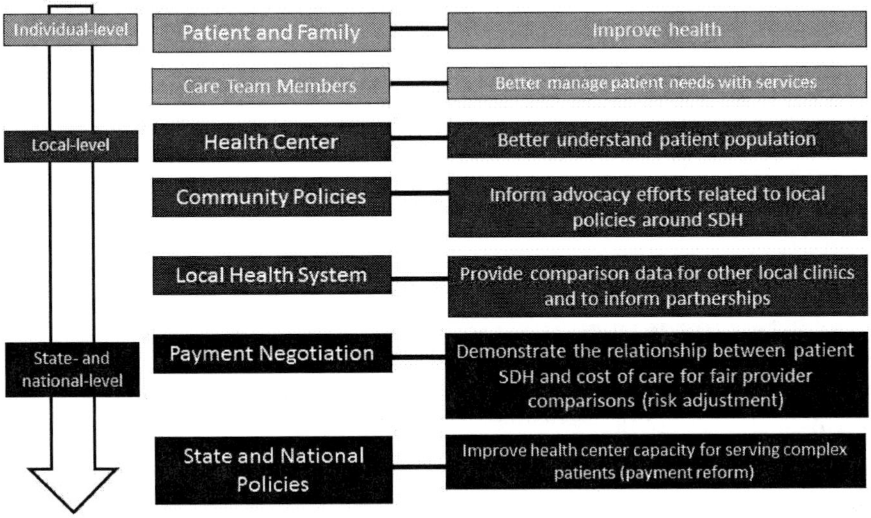


**FIGURE 4-1** Goals of PRAPARE.
NOTE: SDH = social determinants of health.
SOURCE: Faldmo presentation, June 6, 2016.

year by about 25,000 unique patients. For the last decade, the center has provided taxi vouchers when a transportation need is identified. (This practice existed long before the social determinants of health project, Faldmo noted.) The vouchers are funded through a foundation associated with the center, and there is an annual fundraising dinner, with some of the funds collected being allotted for taxi vouchers. The center is also in discussions with the regional transit authority to form a more formal partnership and hopefully provide more than just taxi vouchers for patients. Faldmo noted that the Siouxland Regional Transit System crosses state lines and reaches out into the rural areas. Three managed Medicaid companies are also active in providing transportation vouchers to patients in need.

The no-show rate for the center is about 20 percent, Faldmo said. At this time, the reason for missing an appointment is not tracked, and it is up to the provider to decide if the patient needs to be contacted and rescheduled. He suggested that the center should be regularly assessing why patients are missing appointments and, if the reason involves transportation needs, what can be done to overcome that barrier. Faldmo also mentioned the need for appropriate metrics to assess the impact of addressing transportation for the patients.

Moving forward, the Siouxland Community Health Center will continue to systematically assess for social determinants of health, including transportation, and document this in the EHR. The center is tracking interventions and the resources needed to address social the determinants of health and to navigate patients to community resources. The center is also working to strengthen relationships with community partners to overcome these determinants, including transportation, which has been identified as a need in the community. The center will identify how many missed appointments are due to lack of transportation and assess, during pre-visit preparation, which patients may have transportation needs for that visit as well as for laboratory testing or any overdue services. Faldmo said that the center wants to be more proactive in assessing the transportation needs before patients even come in, rather than waiting for them to not show up. Finally, the center will be working with the Siouxland Regional Transit System to identify additional ways to help patients.

The PRAPARE project to assess social determinants of health is just scratching the surface, Faldmo concluded, and transportation is a big part of the project, and community partnership is critical. Addressing the social determinants of health, Faldmo added, is also an essential part of moving from volume-based care to value-based care.

## HEALTHTRAN

To help address the transportation component of health care access in rural areas, the Missouri Foundation for Health provided the Missouri Rural Health Association with a $500,000 grant over a 3-year period to examine ways to span the gap. This led to the launch of the HealthTran pilot program, which began as a cross-sector collaboration between the Missouri Rural Health Association and the Missouri Public Transit Association and now includes the state primary care association and local health care and transportation organizations. HeathTran serves 10 counties in rural southcentral Missouri that span nearly 8,000 square miles. The total population of the 10 counties is about 290,000 people, Alewine said, or less than 37 people per square mile. There is no major metropolitan area in that part of the state, she continued, and most people receive care at a rural tertiary hospital in the Ozarks community of West Plains, a small city of less than 15,000 people. There is a significant amount of poverty in the area and a lack of good economic opportunities and jobs. The public transit infrastructure in Missouri is woefully inadequate statewide, Alewine said, and most of the state funding goes to the two large metropolitan areas of the state. State funding for the rural areas is limited, she said, and thus FTA funding is important for rural areas.

The HealthTran pilot was designed to gather high-quality data to support the theory that transportation does, in fact, improve patient health; to use that data to advocate for increased transportation funding at the state and federal levels to improve health care access and patient outcomes; and to create a sustainable and replicable program. The program is patient-centric, putting the needs of the patient/rider first. HealthTran coordinators serve as the interface between patients and the public transit providers in the region, scheduling transportation for the patients. Alewine said that at this time HealthTran uses public transit providers exclusively and advocates for increased public transit services (i.e., models involving private or volunteer transportation have not been used at this point).

Getting rides for patients is making a big difference, Alewine said, not only in the quality of life, but also in health care and health outcomes. She echoed the concerns of previous speakers, emphasizing the costs of missed appointments. An initial study at the start of HealthTran found that 20 percent of missed appointments were attributed to a lack of transportation. She pointed out that for a provider who schedules 20 patients per day at an average charge of $150 dollars each, the missed appointments will result in a loss of $3,000 per week, or an entire day's worth of potential billable revenue. A round-trip ride ranges from $20 to $50, depending on the need of the patient (e.g., mobile patient, stretcher transport). If the average round trip ride is $30, the total cost of getting 20 patients to their appointments is $600 dollars. This is a 1:5 gross return on investment relative to the charge for the visit (compared to the ride cost). Assuming the provider nets 70 percent of the charges, the expected reimbursement would be $105. This type of data helps to make the case for transportation with health care partners, Alewine said.

In addition to the revenue for providers when patients get to their care appointments, which Alewine noted is a cost to the payers, there is also a significant benefit in terms of avoided ED visits and inpatient admissions. HealthTran is now engaging payers to gain access to patient-specific claims data in order to further understand and enhance the business case for including transportation as a component of benefits packages. Alewine said that it is a challenge to show the financial benefits to the health care system of getting patients to care and to present a mechanism for providers to invest in transportation for their patients without raising Anti-Kickback Statute and Stark Law (self-referral) concerns for Medicare and Medicaid patients. She added that the Missouri Rural Health Association is waiting on an advisory opinion on this issue from the Office of the Inspector General. Federally qualified health centers have a safe harbor under the Anti-Kickback Statute, she explained, which allows them to partner in transportation arrangements.

Of the HealthTran riders thus far in the pilot (380 people taking 3,735 scheduled trips), 55 percent are covered by Medicare, 34 percent are covered by Medicaid (Alewine clarified that HealthTran does not provide nonemergency medical transport), 18 percent are uninsured, 13 percent have private insurance, 5 percent have veteran benefits, and 3 percent are veterans but without benefits. Most interesting, she said, are the numbers of trips by riders. Thirty-three percent of riders have taken one scheduled trip, 13 percent have ridden twice, 20 percent have ridden 3 to 9 times, and 25 percent have taken 10 or more rides to get to their care (e.g., patients with multiple, chronic issues).

The HealthTran model is designed around the patient, Alewine reiterated, and is designed to be sustainable. The cycle begins when the patient seeks care and says he or she has a transportation barrier. Alewine said that the clinic front office staff are being trained to ask whether patients have a ride to their next appointment. Patients in need of transportation are referred to HealthTran, then a coordinator facilitates the transportation through one of a variety of channels, and the patient is transported. The entire model is based on the ability to create a data-supported case demonstrating the value of transportation to the health care system. The next step, which HealthTran is still working on, is for the health care provider to realize a return on investment and share a percentage of that return with HealthTran so the cycle can continue. HealthTran is collecting data on the costs of patient rides and the billable cost for their care. The transportation and health care systems are valuable to each other, especially in rural areas, she concluded. Using data to demonstrate the financial value is the only way to achieve policy change. Alewine referred participants to the Missouri Rural Health Association website for additional data and reports on HealthTran.

## CHILDREN'S HEALTH FUND

The Children's Health Fund is dedicated to meeting the health care needs of children at risk. Founded in 1987, the Children's Health Fund supports a network of pediatric care programs in 14 states and the District of Columbia, each in affiliation with a major teaching hospital or community health center. Johnson explained that more than 50 mobile clinics serving more than 300 sites totaling more than 275,000 visits per year, for a total of more than 3.6 million health encounters with children and families since inception. The Children's Health Fund uses what it learns in its clinical programs to inform its policy and advocacy work to effect change, specifically, to get children into medical homes and help overcome barriers to health for medically underserved children and families.

### Transportation as a Health Access Barrier

The lack of transportation is a critical health access barrier for children, Johnson said, although this fact was not obvious at first, even in a mobile care model. The role of transportation first came to light in the homeless program in New York City. Children living in the shelters were seen in the mobile clinic and referred for specialty care in the Bronx. Although New York City has an extensive public transportation system, the adherence rate for children completing specialty care appointments was very low (around 10 percent), and it was determined that transportation was a significant barrier. Once transportation assistance was provided, adherence rose to nearly 70 percent.

Following the passage of the Children's Health Insurance Program (CHIP) in the late 1990s, the Children's Health Fund mounted a National Child Health Caravan, which delivered two Children's Health Fund mobile medical units to the Mississippi Delta region and staged a series of town hall meetings along the route from New York to the Gulf Coast. At every one of those town hall meetings, Johnson said, a significant number of community residents said they were aware of CHIP and had enrolled their children but faced transportation barriers to getting to care. This prompted the Children's Health Fund to develop a health transportation shortage index tool[3] and to conduct a series of national and regional surveys to determine where there was transportation disadvantage across states and communities and who would require extra support to get to health appointments. Through the development of programs, partnerships, and advocacy efforts, the Children's Health Fund is committed to working within its network to improve transportation access and to help ensure that medical appointments are being kept.

Johnson highlighted several of the implications of transportation as a health access barrier, particularly for medically underserved children, including missed opportunities for immunizations and routine well-child care; an increased incidence of untreated chronic illnesses (e.g., asthma); an increased use of EDs (and ambulances) for nonemergency care; and an increase in preventable hospitalizations.

Johnson described the results a study of EDs in the Mississippi Delta that found, again, that transportation is a barrier to keeping health care appointments (Grant et al., 2010). Even in communities where working families had a car, that car was often unavailable, generally because it was being used to transport a parent to work, and any routine child health care had to be postponed until that car was available. All (100 percent) of the interviewees in the study reported having missed a child's health care appointment during the preceding 12 months because of transportation, and all of those respondents were after-hours ED users. The study concluded that non-urgent pediatric ED use could be reduced by extending

[3] Discussed further by Grant in Chapter 6.

clinic hours, adding a walk-in service, and making transportation more available.

The bottom line, Johnson said, is that transportation is a key element of the "enhanced medical home" model of care and that transportation accessibility, promotion, and use will contribute to improved health outcomes for children and families. There is a tremendous potential value in a collaboration between the health and transportation sectors, he said. There is the potential for improved return on investment in terms of health costs, health outcomes, and the ability of infrastructure to provide the intended services. There are also opportunities to leverage technological innovation and for local economic development in underserved communities.

### Transportation for Community Health Initiative

Transportation for Community Health is a strategic initiative to identify and reduce the impact of transportation barriers, to mobilize and engage key community leaders and stakeholders, and to focus on collaborative planning that incorporates community-based perspectives. The initiative is informed by integrated health and transportation sector data. It is focused on two very rural, very medically underserved counties in the interior of Mississippi, and it is partnering with the Mississippi Department of Transportation, the Community Transportation Association of America, the Sunflower-Humphreys Counties Progress, Inc., and others.

The proposed framework includes a needs analysis using the health transportation shortage index tool to geomap the state and identify areas of transportation disadvantage, Johnson said. Current data suggest that 65 percent of Mississippi counties (53 of 82) are at high risk for transportation shortages. A governance and oversight framework will be established, and the appropriate management coordination model to address the needs will be determined. The initiative will also identify potential resources, and strategize regarding ongoing sustainability. Finally, Johnson said, it will be important to determine the metrics for evaluation.

Johnson outlined some of the key elements of the Transportation for Community Health initiative. The initiative is a collaboration of national, state, and local partners; it cultivates local leadership; it builds on a shared understanding of how health access is shaped by a set of social determinants; it prioritizes establishing community trust as a key to progress in planning and decision-making processes; it recognizes that there are likely resource limitations; it encourages innovative approaches to mitigate; and it includes an early periodic screening, diagnosis, and treatment plan for evaluating success (based on a set of core screening benefits embedded within Medicaid for children).

Some of the lessons learned thus far from the Transportation for Community Health initiative, as outlined by Johnson, include

- The importance of establishing **trust** by aligning with anchor organizations that have a track record of success in convening community stakeholders.
- The irreplaceable value of **momentum** that is stakeholder generated and progress that is driven through local leadership.
- The critical need for strategic planning that recognizes that success will likely be **incremental and nonlinear.**
- Success in forging relationships and "moving the needle" in economically disadvantaged, underserved communities is **hard won.** There is often a degree of residual disaffection related to previous attempts to engage by non-local institutions.
- **Investment in appropriate relationship building** and outreach is necessary to encourage and support community stakeholders to engage, discuss, and take action on basic infrastructure issues that can improve access, opportunities, and outcomes for their community.

In closing, Johnson offered some questions for further discussion among participants. Do health sector (especially community-based) providers participate in the transportation planning process in your state and county? Should they be invited? How can this be incentivized? How can transportation be incorporated as a quality measure in the contractual process with managed care providers? How can we best make the case for the value of transportation services within the transforming health system? Innovation and new technologies are changing the face of health care delivery and transportation. Can this be a driver for collaboration?

## DISCUSSION

Panelists, discussants, and participants discussed a variety of issues following the presentations. Topics included developing a relationship with the state DOT; cost sharing; making the case for the role of transportation in patient outcomes; and funding, regulatory, and other challenges.

### Developing a Relationship with the State DOT

Carr prompted panelists to describe their relationship with the state DOT and how that relationship has helped to improve and sustain the examples discussed. Alewine said that HealthTran originally partnered with the two large rural public transit organizations in Missouri: OATS, and Southeast Missouri Transportation Service. Through that partnership, the Missouri Department of Transportation (MoDOT) was brought to the table. As HealthTran has evolved, so has the relationship, she said, and the organizations are still learning the best ways to work together to support each other. She said that HealthTran just submitted an application for Rides to Wellness funding in partnership with MoDOT.

Faldmo said that the Siouxland Community Health Center is just starting its relationship with the Siouxland Regional Transit System and is working to partner with it and to formalize the relationship. Kell said that Pathways has done much of its work thus far within the counties, but is now at the point where cross-county assistance is needed, and it will be reaching out to develop a more formal relationship with the (state and local) DOT.

Carr emphasized the importance of cooperation, relationships, and establishing trust when working with a DOT to provide better outcomes for patients. He encouraged participants to work with their state DOT and said that, in most states, nonurban funding and specialized transportation funding goes through the DOT.

## Cost Sharing

Carr recalled the discussion of bus passes and vouchers by panelists and asked about other cost-sharing efforts between the transportation and health care communities that have been successful. Kell responded that for Pathways to Better Health of the Lakeshore, the health system is funding the bus passes and vouchers along with covering the patients and has negotiated a fair contract with the transit authority at reduced cost. Costs are being shared among all three parties—the patient, the health care system, and the transit system.

For HealthTran, Alewine said, although there is no formal arrangement, rural public transit has stepped up with reduced-price options for patients who do not have rides. The health care partners are now in the process of developing a membership type model, and HealthTran will be able to pay for some transportation through a grant.

Faldmo reiterated that PRAPARE is in the preliminary stages, and health center leaders are looking to see if they can discount transportation costs for patients further through a formal contract with the DOT.

Conrick referred participants to the CTAA webpage where they can learn more about the work of CTAA with regard to health care transportation, and to learn about the solutions health care grantees have submitted.[4]

### The Role of Transportation and Patient Outcomes

Conrick raised the issue of encouraging the health care system to recognize the importance of transportation in patient outcomes. She observed that the *International Classification of Diseases*, ICD-10, now has several billable codes for transportation.

Kell pointed out that while Medicare is consistent nationwide, each state includes billable codes as part of its state Medicaid plan amendments, and every state is a little bit different. She noted that there are examples that indicate that the health care system is recognizing that transportation is significant. For instance, in addition to transportation being part of the Medicaid benefit in Michigan, community health workers teach beneficiaries how to use the benefit because many do not understand it. She highlighted the need to determine which efforts are most effective in helping patients use their transportation benefit and then start replicating best practices to achieve more systemic utilization on a national level.

Faldmo also reiterated the need for data and expressed optimism at the work of the National Association of Community Health Centers with PRAPARE to quantify the need for transportation to health care.

Johnson suggested that the uptake on the health side has been far less robust than it could be and that the transportation sector seems more aware of the need. As the health system is transformed, it is the demonstration of savings to the system that will help make the case for transportation.

Alewine highlighted the need to bring the payers into the discussions and suggested that value-based incentives could help to increase the attention to transportation for patients by health care providers.

### Challenges

Participants discussed overcoming the funding, regulatory, and other challenges of bringing health care and transportation together. Stock provided a brief background on the FTA Section 5311 program (49 U.S.C. 5311), the Formula Grants for Rural Areas program through which the FTA funds public transit in rural areas. The funding is limited; Stock said that the total is about $600 million nationwide per year. She expressed hope

[4] For information about CTAA programs on medical transportation, see http://web1.ctaa.org/webmodules/webarticles/anmviewer.asp?a=16&z=40 (accessed September 22, 2016). For information about grantee submissions of innovative transportation solutions, see http://nationalcenterformobilitymanagement.org/challenge (accessed August 4, 2016).

that the program would grow in the future, as the current level of funding does not come close to meeting the full need for public transit in rural areas.

Alewine said that one challenge has been waiting for delayed funds. For example, she said that Section 5310 dollars were expected to be awarded in January, but that due to issues on the FTA side of the process, the Missouri Rural Health Association was still waiting on contracts. The biggest barrier currently, she said, is the procurement process, which she described as "incredibly daunting" for smaller organizations to navigate. The association is working with the state DOT to address this barrier and to find a better and a faster way to do procurement that meets rules and requirements and does not have the hurdles.

Phillips briefly described the work of the National Rural Transit Assistance Program (RTAP). The program is a hub for knowledge management, gathering information from transit operators, and providing training that is specific to the transit operator's needs. Every 2 years the National RTAP conducts a survey of rural transit operators and FTA program managers at the state level. She said that one of the issues for rural transit providers is funding, and she observed that health care organizations often do not understand the way that financing is done for rural transit (e.g., there is often a lack of state matching funds). Rural transit also often involves transporting one person at a time to a distant medical appointment, which is more costly than transporting several people at once. She stressed the need for communication and sharing quality information as well as the importance of partnerships and relationships between the provider of health care services and the provider of transportation services. It is also important to consider the environment being served and to use common sense. For example, people who are transit-dependent should be having dialysis on Monday, Wednesday, and Friday, when transit is running, instead of Tuesday, Thursday, Saturday, as many rural transit systems do not run on Saturday. Technology can help with communication and providing transit services when and where they are needed.

Sneha Peck of America's Essential Hospitals asked about the role of the hospital or health system in initiating the transportation conversation and ensuring long-term sustainability for programs. Kell suggested that the process starts with the hospital's community needs assessment and the community health improvement plan prepared with the health department. A challenge, however, is getting sufficient community participation in the community needs assessment plans and processes.

# 5

# Report Back from Breakout Groups

Following the first two panel sessions, participants divided into two breakout groups for more in-depth discussion of data from several case examples of transportation projects. After reconvening in plenary session, breakout facilitators Michelle Proser, the director of research at the National Association of Community Health Centers, and Art Guzzetti of the American Public Transit Association, briefly described the presentations and discussions that took place in their groups. (Highlights are presented in Box 5-1.)

## WASHINGTON, DC

One of the breakout groups heard presentations of data from two projects in the Washington, DC, area. The first presentation, Linking Transportation, Health, and the Built Environment in Washington, DC, was given by Anneta Arno, the director of the Office of Health Equity in the Office of the Director of the District of Columbia Department of Health; Raka Choudhury, the citywide transportation planner at the Progressive Transportation Services Administration at the District (of Columbia) Department of Transportation (DDOT); and Steve Strauss, the deputy associate director of the Progressive Transportation Services Administration at DDOT. The second presentation, Efficient and Effective Provision of Mobility to Health Care, was given by Steve Yaffe, the transit services manager for Arlington County, Virginia.

**BOX 5-1**
**Highlights and Main Points Made by Individual Speakers and Participants**[a]

- Data are essential for knowing who the patients/riders are and for demonstrating the value of transportation to health care outcomes. However, there are barriers to data sharing across sectors and inconsistency in data collection across systems. (Proser)
- The intent of interagency collaboration on transportation to health-related activities is not transformation in just one sector, but transformation of communities to achieve increased vitality and efficiencies. (Proser)
- Health centers have expressed willingness to participate in trip scheduling at the time of appointment scheduling if it is simple for them. Smart software solutions are needed, and implementation issues (e.g., billing, eligibility rules, cost, time) need to be solved in advance and might require policy reforms. (Guzzetti)
- To compensate for unreliable transportation systems, some health centers appear to be building in buffer time around appointments, which is potentially wasted and costly time. (Stewart)

[a] This list is the rapporteurs' summary of the main points made by individual speakers and participants (noted in parentheses) and does not reflect any consensus among workshop participants or endorsement by the National Academies of Sciences, Engineering, and Medicine.

## Data

Proser reported that, in addition to hearing about the different models and innovations, much of the time in his group was spent discussing the importance of data for knowing who the patients/riders are and for demonstrating the value of transportation to health care outcomes. Participants discussed how best to demonstrate the value in interagency collaboration, with an emphasis on demonstrating the value together. The intent is not transformation in just one sector, but transformation of communities to achieve increased vitality and efficiencies.

Some of the data challenges discussed included the general lack of data sharing across sectors and various barriers to data sharing, such as restrictions on sharing personal health information under the Health Insurance Portability and Accountability Act (HIPAA). It was also noted that data collection is inconsistent across different hospital systems, even within the same community. Although all not-for-profit hospital systems are conducting community needs assessments, they are not using the same measures or benchmarking the same issues and problems, making it harder to have cross-community collaboration on the findings.

The need to have data to better understand who the consumers are was also raised, Proser reported. Can data be used to better segment patients with transportation needs? For example, it was suggested that the increase in the number of patients who are using public transportation programs could be due to the increase in chronic disease.

To address the HIPAA barriers, there have been attempts to create central hubs for data sharing, collaboration, and coordination of services. Several participants emphasized the need for better data on the health care side as well as the need for greater consistency across the community health needs assessments. It was also observed that there are many different efforts to provide transportation for different groups (i.e., different disease categories), and many participants discussed the need to identify areas of intersection and reduce overlaps in order to create more efficiency.

### Costs

Participants in the breakout group discussed costs, Proser reported, and also the importance of being good stewards of resources. Several participants also highlighted the need to reframe how the case is presented in order to effectively demonstrate the return on investment of getting patients to care. It is a challenging conversation, Proser acknowledged, because the utilization of primary preventive and chronic care is increasing, but there are long-term benefits, such as lower utilization of acute care and an increased vitality of communities. There is a cost associated with improved outcomes in the short term, but there are potential savings in the long term.

### Defining Success

Population health improvement, a better quality of life, and improved well-being are all measures of success. It was noted, however, that social interactions and general well-being are not captured in clinical care. Cost savings were also discussed as a measure of success, especially cost savings that result from maximizing efficiencies through prevention. As more and more patients are dealing with preventable chronic illness (e.g., end-stage renal disease), providers of both health care and transportation are now seeing how the social barriers to health affect outcomes and costs.

In closing, Proser reiterated the power of data for demonstrating value and the need to work collaboratively across sectors. Data is advocacy, she said, and can help us to understand specific community needs and identify where to reinvest any savings generated upstream.

## BOSTON, MASSACHUSETTS

The other breakout group heard presentations of data from two projects in the Boston, Massachusetts, area. The first presentation, Smart Transit for Health Care, was given by Moumita Dasgupta, a principal investigator in the Department of Physics and Astronomy at Amherst College, and Sarah Anderson, the business development manager at Cambridge Systematics, Inc. The second presentation, Comparing Scheduled and Actual Transit Accessibility to Health Centers, was given by Anson Stewart, a Ph.D. candidate in the Interdepartmental Transportation Program at the Massachusetts Institute of Technology. Two main points emerged from the presentations, Guzzetti reported: the need to optimize appointment trip scheduling, and the importance of reliability.

### Scheduling Trips

The first presentation described how geocoded addresses revealed that low-income populations are lacking health care access relative to the rest of the population. The proposed solution was to schedule the necessary transportation at the same time that the patient calls to schedule the health appointment, so that both needs are addressed at once. It was noted that health centers have expressed a willingness to participate in this approach if it is simple for them (e.g., through using smart software). Several participants discussed the need to resolve questions and address challenges in advance. Issues with billing, eligibility rules, cost, time, and expertise are all solvable, Guzzetti said, but might require policy reforms.

### Reliability

The second presentation considered the issue of reliability. The research that was presented had found that two-thirds of bus riders reported arriving late for or missing an appointment at least once within the preceding year. Stewart explained that the research hypothesis was that there would be a positive correlation between unreliability and missed appointments. The expectation was that more people would be missing appointments at health care centers, for which general transit accessibility is often less reliable. The preliminary findings, however, were the opposite. Health care centers, which by a certain measure have more unreliable transit, actually had fewer people reporting missed appointments. One preliminary theory to explain that observation is that those health care clinics are building in "reliability buffer time" because they expect the trips are going to be unreliable. There may actually be wasted reliability buffer time built into every trip, Steward said, and he suggested that this would be important to quantify.

Another topic of discussion, Guzzetti reported, was the relative reliability of other transportation options (e.g., highways). Several participants in the breakout group also considered what the social response to this unreliability might be—for example, improving the capacity and reliability of transit.

## DISCUSSION

### Payers

In response to a question from a webcast participant, Ysela Llort, planning committee chair, prompted participants for comments on the engagement of payers in transportation issues. Meadows responded that, despite recent progress, there is still a disconnect between transportation and payers, especially relative to Medicaid. He said that Geisinger is looking at developing a concierge service, so that if a patient is turned down by the Medical Assistance Transportation Program in Pennsylvania (discussed in Chapter 3), that patient can call the concierge service and arrange a ride to his or her appointment. Meadows also mentioned recent interest from a provider in making a change to its bundled payment methodology, so that the cost of the transportation would be covered as part of the bundle. This is a step in the right direction as well, he said.

Stacy Elmer from Kaiser Permanente in Southern California said that Kaiser often considers transportation to be either medically necessary or something that is a covered benefit. She added that Kaiser in Southern California is working to better meet the needs of its members in terms of transportation and to better understand why patients are missing appointments.

Flora Castillo, the vice president of community and strategic engagement at UnitedHealthcare and a volunteer board member of New Jersey Transit, said that UnitedHealthcare is working to create innovative partnerships with the transportation sector to ensure that United is addressing the needs of members. Castillo referred participants to a recently released white paper by UnitedHealthcare in which a framework is proposed for measuring the quality of care delivered in a managed, long-term services and supports environment.[1] Within those measures are several questions on transportation, she added. Castillo said that UnitedHealthcare is interested in conducting more pilot programs, and she encouraged participants to discuss ideas with her.

---

[1] Available at https://www.uhccommunityandstate.com/content/dam/community-state/PDFs/NAB_LTSS_Whitepaper.pdf (accessed August 4, 2016).

### Software

A number of workshop participants discussed further the potential of software for trip and appointment planning, and it was suggested that one function of such software could be to immediately contact a patient if he or she does not show up for an appointment in order to find out what the issue is and to assist. Another function of the software could be to find transportation options for getting back home for patients who do make it to their appointments. A participant noted the potential of application programming interfaces and open-source systems using standardized data. An advantage of this collaborative approach is that an improvement made anywhere is shared with the community using that software.

# 6

# Data Sources and Tools for Understanding and Addressing Health-Related Transportation Needs

In this session, panelists described a range of data sources, tools, and ongoing activities that could be useful in helping define the transportation-to-health issue, make the case for funding support, and develop patient-centric solutions.[1] Chris Barnett, the co-director of the Center for Applied Research and Environmental Systems (CARES) at the University of Missouri at Columbia, described the Community Commons, a website providing access to numerous datasets and tools for mapping, analysis, and reporting. Roy Grant, a public health research consultant who was formerly at the Children's Health Fund, discussed using data to demonstrate the extent of the problem of lack of transportation and to plan solutions to improve health care access. Marcie Cynamon, the director of the Division of Health Interview Statistics for the National Center for Health Statistics (NCHS) at the Centers for Disease Control and Prevention, provided a brief overview of the National Health Interview Survey. Kelsey Walter, the director of National Core Indicators-Aging and Disabilities (NCI-AD) at the National Association of States United for Aging and Disabilities (NASUAD), described the NCI-AD survey and shared preliminary results relative to transportation and health care. Finally, Karen White, the director of the Office of Statistical and Economic Analysis in the Bureau of Transportation Statistics (BTS) at the U.S. Department of Transportation, highlighted three BTS areas of focus related to health and accessibility: safety, clean air and connectivity, and active transportation.

[1] The many resources and websites shared throughout the workshop are collated in Appendix C.

**BOX 6-1**
**Highlights and Main Points Made by Individual Speakers and Participants[a]**

- Collaboration hubs can help to facilitate the sharing of data, maps, reports strategies, best practices, presentations, personal stories, and organizational information, and to foster conversations across groups. (Barnett)
- Together, geographic information system and U.S. Census data can be powerful tools to identify potentially vulnerable subpopulations and areas at risk for transportation-related access barriers, and also to inform the development of solutions. (Barnett, Grant)
- While it is important to predict where the needs will be, it is also critical to strengthen infrastructure to meet those needs, and to improve public transit availability and usability. (Grant)
- There is a need to develop standardized definitions for assessing data across agencies and sectors. (Grant)
- Pilot programs are one way to demonstrate the impact of transportation on health outcomes. Large health systems, such as Kaiser, are well suited to conduct such studies as they have patient-level data over long periods of time. Pilot studies could potentially be funded under a variety of federal grant opportunities (e.g., Federal Transit Administration Section 5310, Fixing America's Surface Transportation Act funding, Mobility on Demand Sandbox). (Elmer, Stock, Valdes, Yaffee, participants)

[a] This list is the rapporteurs' summary of the main points made by individual speakers and participants (noted in parentheses) and does not reflect any consensus among workshop participants or endorsement by the National Academies of Sciences, Engineering, and Medicine.

The presentations were followed by comments from discussants Steve Yaffe, a transit services manager with Arlington Transit; David Riley, the director of the Veterans Transportation Program at the U.S. Department of Veterans Affairs; and Peter McNichol, the chief of quality control for non-emergency medical transportation at the Department of Vermont Health Access. The session was moderated by Catherine Lawson, an associate professor of geography and planning at the State University of New York at Albany, and Paul Hughes-Cromwick, the co-director of the Center for Sustainable Health Spending at the Altarum Institute. (Highlights are presented in Box 6-1.)

## COMMUNITY COMMONS

Community Commons is a website supporting dialogue to improve communities and inspire change through group-based discovery, discussion, and shared resources, grounded in data and analytical tools that can lead to positive change in communities, Barnett said. It is a joint effort among CARES; the University of Missouri, which provides the data and technical support; the nonprofit group IP3, which handles the stewardship, marketing, and user support aspects of the project; and Community Initiatives in Portland, Oregon, which does much of the community-based work and relationships. At the core of Community Commons is a national Web-based geographic information system (GIS). The website provides access to thousands of datasets that are available for mapping (from a variety of mainly public sources) as well as supporting analysis and reporting tools. The available information spans a variety of topics, Barnett said, such as education, environment, food, housing, economics, poverty, health, emergency management, transportation, and demographics.

Barnett shared an example of how one might use Community Commons (see Figure 6-1). By first mapping predominant race/ethnicity by U.S. Census block group using data from the 2010 U.S. Census, one can interact

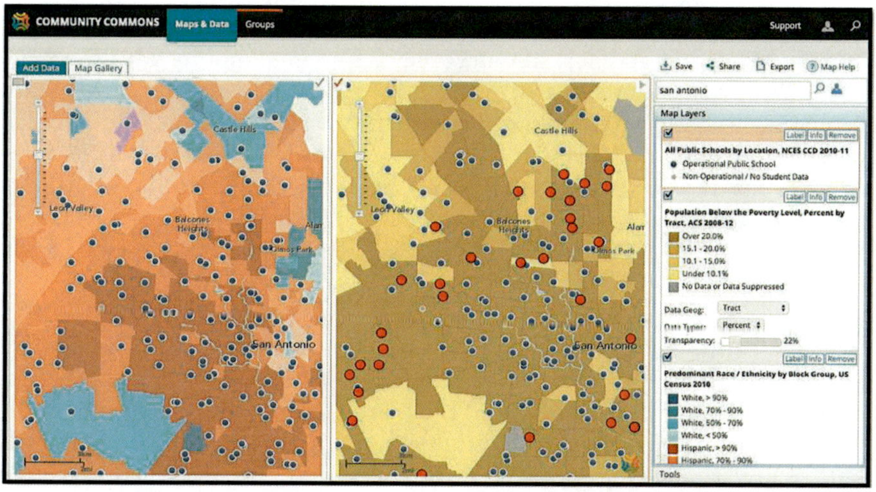


**FIGURE 6-1** Maps showing predominant race/ethnicity (left) and population below poverty level (right), both displaying public school information to demonstrate the intersection. The database was then queried for schools with more than 90 percent of students receiving free and reduced price lunch, which are shown in red on the poverty map. Data for each school can then be accessed for further analysis, and downloaded.
SOURCES: Barnett presentation, June 7, 2016; Public Schools with Poverty and Predominant Race/Ethnicity, San Antonio Area, Texas, USA. Community Commons (2016). Retrieved April 2016, www.communitycommons.org.

with the national map and zoom to a specific city or area. One can then view the spatial distribution of specific characteristics of U.S. Census block groups on the map and access the associated data. Subsets of data can be queried for analysis and used for further exploration and visualization within Community Commons or downloaded for further analysis outside Community Commons. Barnett said that those who register to use the maps and data on the system can save all of the maps they generate to their account and return to them at any time for additional analysis, without having to start again from the beginning with data selection.

Beyond the core data engine and mapping tools, Community Commons provides tools and visualizations that help to provide meaning to data. Barnett highlighted four tools as examples. The Vulnerable Populations Footprint tool uses public data to provide a snapshot of where in the community some of the most vulnerable populations reside by mapping the intersection of poverty and low education. Users can adjust thresholds levels to define areas of greatest concern and create a vulnerable populations demographic report. Another tool is the Location Opportunity Footprint, which maps the intersection of good schools, nearby jobs, and low housing and transportations costs. The tool uses data released by the U.S. Department of Housing and Urban Development (HUD), and the U.S. Environmental Protection Agency, among others. The Community Health Needs Assessment tool is intended to provide a base set of secondary health and demographic data for launching a community health needs assessment. The tool also includes dial charts and maps that provide some state and national context for the results. The last example was the Local Food Market Report, which is designed to encourage and support local food producers.

## Collaboration Hubs

One of the more powerful aspects of Community Commons, Barnett said, is the ability for users to participate in a collaboration hub, moving beyond the data into carrying on "the conversation among partners working to improve communities." Within a hub, a group can upload and share data, maps, reports strategies, best practices, and presentations and tell its stories to help get the organization's point across. Hubs can interact with other hubs and foster conversations across different platforms and groups within Community Commons. Some groups, he said, also embed information from Community Commons on their own websites to leverage the power of Community Commons within their own area. Barnett encouraged participants to visit the website to learn more.[2]

---

[2] See http://www.communitycommons.org (accessed August 4, 2016).

## HEALTH TRANSPORTATION SHORTAGE INDEX

Speaking from his experience at the Children's Health Fund, Grant described using data to demonstrate the extent of the problem of lack of transportation and to plan solutions to improve health care access. A series of national surveys made it clear that there are areas of the country (e.g., areas of high poverty, rural areas) that are much more affected by lack of transportation than other areas. Targeted data collection (in 2006 and 2010, before passage of the Patient Protection and Affordable Care Act) showed that 39 percent of U.S. residents did not have public transportation available in their community, 11 percent of households did not own a working vehicle, and only 42 percent of those with public transportation in their community reported it could be used to get to a heath care site (ranging from 14 percent in rural areas to 69 percent in major cities). Automobile ownership did not vary significantly across the range from big cities through suburban, small town, and rural areas, while access to public transit declined steeply from big cities to less densely populated areas.

The Children's Health Fund was interested in missed pediatric appointments, and surveys found that 4 percent of U.S. children had missed a health care appointment within the preceding 12 months because transportation was not available. This rose to 9 percent in households with incomes less than $50,000. Thirty-one percent reported seeking care in the emergency department (ED) later for the condition associated with the missed appointment. Applying U.S. Census data to this observation, Grant implies that there are 1 million potentially preventable pediatric ED visits annually.

Those data were used to develop an index to target areas at high risk for transportation-related access barriers, Grant said. The Health Transportation Shortage Index (HTSI, see Figure 6-2) is a validated tool for health planning that assesses factors associated with transit barriers to primary care access and generates a point score from 0 to 11.[3] A score of greater than 7 indicates high risk, he said. The factors assessed include rural/metro status, poverty rate (proxy for the likelihood of not owning a vehicle), health professional shortages, safety net health clinics, and public transportation resources. Grant noted that one criterion for the selection of the data was that the data be readily available and not difficult to obtain, which led to such decisions as using the poverty rate of an area instead of car ownership data.

GIS software was then used to map by longitude and latitude the safety clinics in each county in a given state (i.e., federally qualified health centers, rural health clinics, safety net hospitals, and local health department

[3] For further information, see http://www.childrenshealthfund.org/sites/default/files/Health-Transportation-Shortage-Index-HTSI.pdf (accessed August 4, 2016).

## The Health Transportation Shortage Index

Rate each of these 5 factors associated with transportation and health care access in points, as indicated, and add the points for the HTSI℠ score. A total score of 6 or higher indicates a transportation shortage area. The higher the score, the higher the risk for transportation-related barriers to child health care access.

### 1 Type of area, based on population (using Census Bureau population data)

| | |
|---|---|
| RURAL<br>POPULATION ≤ 5,000 | 4 points |
| SMALL TOWN<br>POPULATION > 5,000 AND ≤ 10,000 | 3 points |
| SMALL CITY<br>POPULATION > 10,000 AND ≤ 20,000 | 2 points |
| URBAN AREA<br>POPULATION > 20,000 AND ≤ 50,000 | 1 point |
| METROPOLITAN AREA<br>POPULATION > 50,000 | 0 points |

### 2* Child poverty rate (% in poverty) exceeds US (using most current available data)

| | |
|---|---|
| YES<br>BY 1.25X OR GREATER | 3 points |
| YES<br>BY LESS THAN 1.25X | 2 points |
| SAME AS US | 1 point |
| LOWER THAN US | 0 points |

### 3 Public transportation availability

| | |
|---|---|
| NONE | 3 points |
| DEMAND-RESPONSE<br>(E.G., PARATRANSIT) | 2 points |
| LIMITED<br>(DOES NOT RUN FULL-TIME AND/OR ROUTES DO NOT COVER TARGET AREA) | 1 point |
| YES | 0 points |

### 4 HPSA designation

| | |
|---|---|
| YES<br>ENTIRE GEOGRAPHIC AREA | 2 points |
| YES<br>PARTIAL GEOGRAPHIC AREA | 1 point |
| NO | 0 points |

### 5 FQHC in area (for high poverty areas; include rural health clinics)

| | |
|---|---|
| NO | 2 points |
| ONE | 1 point |
| TWO OR MORE | 0 points |
| NOT APPLICABLE<br>(NOT A HIGH POVERTY AREA) | 0 points |

*** NOTES:**

1. There is a strong negative correlation between poverty and automobile ownership (i.e., higher poverty rate is associated with lower personal vehicle ownership). The HTSI℠ incorporates personal vehicle ownership through the poverty factor as a component of assessing available transportation resources.

2. If child poverty rate is not available for an area, family or household poverty rates may be used as representative because of the strong correlation among these three indicators.

**FIGURE 6-2** Health Transportation Shortage Index.
NOTE: FQHC = federally qualified health center; HPSA = health professional shortage area; HTSI = Health Transportation Shortage Index.
SOURCES: Grant presentation, June 7, 2016; Children's Health Fund, 2012.

clinics). Population was mapped by U.S. Census block, and straight-line distance was calculated from the population-weighted center to the nearest clinic. An example from Tennessee shared by Grant showed how clinics were well located relative to population centers. Fifty-two percent of counties in Tennessee were identified as high-risk for transportation barriers to health care access; these were generally rural and with higher poverty. Grant said that there was considerable overlap between these counties and areas with shortages of health professionals.

With regard to transportation resources, all high-risk counties in Tennessee had public transit, and 80 percent had paratransit services. The distance to clinics did not differ between high-risk counties and other counties. Furthermore, the straight-line distance to a clinic for residents in most high-risk, high-poverty counties was found to be less than 10 miles. In other words, the majority of the population could be accommodated with vehicular transportation within a 10-mile radius of a safety net clinic, which did not sound like an insurmountable problem, Grant said. Many patients were located within 5 miles of a clinic. A literature search was done of effective strategies to leverage paratransit resources to improve health care access, and several models with proven track records were identified. These included modifying paratransit services to include scheduled stops linking health care sites with population centers, developing contracts between county or state governments and paratransit providers specifically for health care access, and using existing paratransit services to strengthen Medicaid nonemergency medical transportation.

## NATIONAL HEALTH INTERVIEW SURVEY

The mission of NCHS, Cynamon said, is to collect objective, nonpartisan, high-quality data on a broad array of health topics to inform the public, Congress, the White House, and others who are interested in health data. It is 1 of 13 federal agencies that have statistics as their core mission. NCHS houses the Vital Registration Statistics System and runs national health surveys. Cynamon provided a brief overview of the National Health Interview Survey. The survey has been continuously in the field since 1957, she said, and its data collection is done by U.S. Census Bureau interviewers in the homes of the non-institutionalized civilian population. Every year confidential interviews are conducted in 35,000 to 45,000 households. The broad mandate of the survey is to collect data on morbidity and mortality, health risk behaviors and protective factors, actions people take to improve their health, how people access health care, barriers to care, what services people utilize, why people do not utilize health care, and health insurance coverage in the United States. The goal is to develop a general sense of the health of the U.S. population. Cynamon said that the results from the survey are linked to other federal records (e.g., HUD data on Section 8 housing, health data from the Centers for Medicare & Medicaid Services, National Death Index data, data from the Medical Expenditures Panel Survey, and Area Health Resources Files from the Health Resources and Services Administration of the U.S. Department of Health and Human Services [HHS]).

Since 1997, Cynamon said, the survey has included one question on whether problems with transportation delayed getting needed medical care, and the number who answered yes has hovered around 2 percent annually for the past two decades. This is just one question, she said, and it does not provide a very accurate reflection of the complex issues related to transportation and accessing care. But, she suggested, combined with data on mobility impairments, cognitive impairments, and other types of disability and limitations of activity, the survey data could be used to obtain a more detailed picture of the types of assistance needed.

The survey questionnaire is currently being redesigned, and the revised version will be introduced in 2018. The health system has changed dramatically since 1997, but the questionnaire has remained fairly stable, Cynamon said. In addition, the length of the interview has increased over time to about an hour and a half, which can be burdensome for some respondents, she said. In determining how to refocus the questionnaire, NCHS is reaching out to the survey user community, which she noted is not just Congress, the White House, and HHS. There are thousands of users across the country, in academia, community health, state health, and elsewhere who use the data for reports, grant applications, program evaluations, and a vast array of other purposes. Examining barriers to care is an important question for the revised survey. Now that insurance coverage is more accessible, what else is preventing people from getting the care they need? Cynamon encouraged participants to visit the National Health Interview Survey webpage, view the information on the 2018 redesign, and provide input, particularly on any aspects of transportation for which data at the national and state levels would be useful.[4]

## NATIONAL CORE INDICATORS-AGING AND DISABILITIES

NASUAD is the membership organization for state agencies working on aging and disability services, Walter said. In 2015, NASUAD launched the NCI-AD initiative in partnership with the Human Services Research Institute. NCI-AD is a quality-of-life survey of older adults and adults with physical disabilities. Walter said that NCI-AD grew out of the National Core Indicators Survey, which is focused on adults with intellectual and

[4] See https://www.cdc.gov/nchs/nhis/2018_quest_redesign.htm (accessed August 4, 2016).

developmental disabilities. NCI-AD focuses on how individuals are being served by their states' long-term services and supports systems, including skilled nursing facilities, Medicaid waivers, Medicaid state plans, managed long-term services and supports populations, state-funded programs, and Older Americans Act programs.

### NCI-AD Survey

The NCI-AD survey gathers information through face-to-face interviews with consumers who are receiving services (or a proxy, if identified). The process includes a pre-survey used to set up the interviews, the collection of background information on demographics and personal characteristics (from state agency administration records and/or the consumer), and interviewer feedback on the survey experience. The consumer survey consists of 89 questions, including both subjective, satisfaction-related questions that can only be answered by the consumer and objective questions that can be answered by the consumer or, if needed, the proxy.

The survey covers a broad range of measures of quality of life that states are interested in, including community participation, choice and decision making about the types of services individuals are receiving, relationships, satisfaction, service care and coordination, access, self-direction of care, work and employment, rights and respect, health care, medications, safety and wellness, everyday living and affordability, planning for future, and control. Thirteen states participated in the first survey in 2015–2016 (survey period June 1–May 31), Walters said, and more are slated to participate in 2016–2017. She shared some of the mid-year results from six states[5] that committed to a shortened data collection period—specifically, the findings related to transportation and health care.

### Mid-Year Results 2015–2016

The types of area that individuals were living in spanned metropolitan, micropolitan, rural, and small town. The majority lived in their own home or in a family home. Eighty-eight percent of the people surveyed (averaged across six states) reported needing help with everyday activities (e.g., grocery shopping, housecleaning), and 71 percent reported needing help with self-care (e.g., bathing, eating, using the bathroom, getting in and out of bed). An average of 62 percent reported being able to do things outside the home when, and with whom, they wanted to. Those who replied that they were not able to do such things were asked why, and transportation

[5] Colorado, Georgia, Maine, Mississippi, New Jersey, North Carolina.

was one of the most common reasons cited for people not being able to get outside of their homes, Walters reported.

When asked specifically about transportation to get to medical appointments, an average of 91 percent of individuals reported that they did have transportation. Walters said that because these are people being served by Medicaid or state programming, transportation is often included in the health care services they are receiving. Fewer individuals (an average of 71 percent) reported having transportation when they wanted to do other things outside of the home (e.g., social activities, religious services). Walters said that the ability to be active outside of the home is part of the larger context of health. An average of 37 percent of respondents reported having a regular dental visit within the past year, and 62 percent reported having had a vision exam within the same period. In response to a question on the subject of overall wellness, an average of 16 percent reported being "in poor health."

States design their own survey samples, Walter said, and they can assess the data by regional level or by specific population (such as the managed care populations, which can be further subgrouped by managed care organization). The intent is to have data that are useful at the local level that can also be included in the NCI-AD national report. Walter referred participants to the NCI-AD website for the 2015–2016 Six State Mid-Year Report and for information on participating.[6]

## BUREAU OF TRANSPORTATION STATISTICS

Like NCHS, BTS is 1 of the 13 federal agencies that have statistics as their core mission. BTS was created to administer the collection, analysis, and reporting of transportation data and to ensure the most cost-effective use of resources to monitor transportation's contributions to the economy, and transportation's implications (e.g., safety, environment). It is a policy-neutral, objective broker of information and is afforded some special abilities to protect the confidentiality of the information it collects. White spoke about three BTS areas of focus related to health and accessibility: safety, clean air, and connectivity and active transportation.

### Safety: Close Calls/Near Miss Data Program

Confidential close-call reporting allows people who see a close-call incident in the transit environment to report it anonymously. All of the information provided is protected from the Freedom of Information Act, White said. A close call is an event that does not rise to the level of an Occu-

[6] See http://nci-ad.org (accessed August 4, 2016).

pational Safety and Health Administration incident and does not result in an injury, but which a worker considers to be dangerous.

As an example, White mentioned the close-call reporting program that allows employees of the Washington Metropolitan Area Transit Authority (WMATA) to report close calls that WMATA and the two transit workers unions would not otherwise know about. Through this program, BTS has received 349 close call reports and developed 55 preventive safety actions (e.g., concave and convex mirrors, better signage). BTS analyzes data and reports trends and patterns back to WMATA, and WMATA uses that information to implement suggested preventative safety measures.

### Clean Air: National Transportation Atlas Database

The National Transportation Atlas Database is a collection of geospatial databases that depict transportation networks; flows of people, goods, vehicles, and craft over the transportation networks; and social, economic, and environmental conditions that affect or are affected by the transportation networks.[7] The atlas is also capable of supporting intermodal network analysis. White noted that while the atlas includes details on what is moving, it does not collect data on why a vehicle took a trip. She highlighted some data items in the atlas that might be of interest to health and transportation including, for example, infrastructure locations, border crossings, passenger facilities, non-attainment areas, the Fatality Analysis Reporting System, hazmat information, and parks.

White observed that "medical tourism" was an aspect of transportation to health care that had not to that point been discussed at the workshop. In the increasingly connected world, more people are traveling far beyond the local environment for care, she said.

### Connectivity and Active Transportation

There are several databases on connectivity and active transport that are relevant to transportation access to health care.[8] The Intermodal Passenger Connectivity Database includes information that allows passengers to find connections from one mode of transport to another in order to complete a trip. It provides geographic coordinates of rail, airport, ferry, and bus terminals. BTS is now working with Federal Transit Administration

---

[7] See http://www.rita.dot.gov/bts/sites/rita.dot.gov.bts/files/publications/national_transportation_atlas_database/index.html (accessed August 4, 2016).

[8] See the BTS Intermodal Transportation Database, available at http://www.rita.dot.gov/bts/data_and_statistics/intermodal_transportation_database.html (accessed August 4, 2016).

(FTA), through the National Transit Database, to collect stop locations and frequency for intra-city bus transit.

The National Household Travel Survey, conducted by BTS and the Federal Highway Administration, gathers trip-related data such as the mode of transportation and the duration, distance, and purpose of a trip. It also gathers demographic, geographic, and economic data. Questions on trip purpose include whether the trip was for a medical or dental appointment, whether a medical condition limits the person's travel, and the length of time the person has had the medical condition. Data are also used to find walkable and bikeable trips.

BTS also gathers airline industry data, including passengers enplaned on U.S. carrier scheduled domestic and international service and on foreign carrier scheduled international service from the United States.

## DISCUSSION

The main topics of discussion following the presentations included the challenges of predicting demand for transportation services, issues around demonstrating the impact of transportation on health outcomes, and linking data from major national surveys.

### Predicting and Measuring Demand

Yaffe raised a concern that the predictive models used to anticipate future Americans with Disabilities Act paratransit-eligible ridership are overly based on overall U.S. Census figures. There is a need to do market segmentation, he suggested, not only to provide a more accurate predictor of demand for paratransit, but also to understand who will need rides to treatments. Grant mentioned a federally funded program involving comprehensive screening to identify those in need of enabling services to get to health care. Although transportation is a service included in the screening, there is a prohibition against using any of the funding to increase the availability of transportation, he said. This is a vehicle-owning country, he said, and the availability of public transit resources in some counties and communities is very limited. There is also a stigma about using public transit. Not only is it important to predict where the needs will be, Grant added, but it is also critical to strengthen infrastructure to meet those needs and to improve public transit availability and usability. This will require reconsidering how funding is allocated, he said. Barnett said that the tools available on Community Commons—and on GISs in general—can sort through a variety of data sources to help identify subpopulations and, for example, display that information in relationship to transportation nodes or the availability of transportation. He suggested that GIS could also be used to identify the congressional district where the need exists (i.e., for advocacy purposes).

McNichol said that Vermont uses predictive modeling and data for a statewide care coordination program that is run through Vermont Medicaid. Although the program is constantly doing its best to get people rides, it is very limited in what it can do with the amount of funding it gets. Currently, the two biggest users of transportation resources are people traveling to adult day services and people going to opioid treatment centers, both in state and across state lines. McNichol added that some people have had issues with personal safety on buses to programs (e.g., assaults). Predictive modeling does not necessarily identify or help to alleviate these growing problems. Yaffe observed that lack of transportation is an issue for a variety of conditions that lead to complications in the absence of treatment (e.g., untreated hypertension or untreated diabetes can lead to kidney failure and potential need for dialysis). There is a need to better understand why patients need to get to the doctor. Lawson and White emphasized that the National Household Travel Survey website has a variety of tools for analysis and the ability to deal with multiple variables.[9]

## Demonstrating the Value of Transportation to Health-Related Destinations

Riley highlighted the challenges of making the business case for transportation to health-related destinations to the leadership of the U.S. Department of Veterans Affairs and also spoke about the need for metrics. He noted that it is not possible to show that a veteran would not have gotten to a care provider without the provided transportation service. When patients do not make it to their appointment, there might be clinical resources already dedicated to that appointment that go to waste. When patients do not have enabling services that allow them to remain in their homes and be independent, they must often move to a higher level of care (e.g., a nursing home), which can be very expensive. Can a return on investment be shown in terms of reductions in the waste of clinical resources or in the time lost by clinicians or in terms of eliminating the need for costly higher level care?

White commented on the challenges of measuring accessibility. BTS has been looking at matching across administrative data as a measure of accessibility at the U.S. Census tract level, she said. For example, BTS has been matching data from the U.S. Department of Agriculture on food deserts

---

[9] See http://nhts.ornl.gov (accessed August 4, 2016).

with data on transportation accessibility in order to better understand how people are eating and getting food in areas that are not well served by a grocery store with fresh fruits and vegetables. BTS is considering a similar analysis on the availability of different tiers of health care. She added that some areas accessible by car have other challenges, such as parking issues.

Grant highlighted the need to develop standardized definitions for assessing data across agencies and sectors. For example, there are many different definitions of terms such as "rural" and boundaries of a specific "community." "Uninsured" is defined differently in different federal household surveys (e.g., a gap in continuity of coverage during a 12-month period, uninsured continuously for 12 months, etc.). The lack of standardized terminology makes getting straight answers to simple questions very difficult, he said.

Stacey Elmer from Kaiser in Southern California suggested that the way to test whether providing transportation improves health outcomes is to use pilot programs. As an example, she described the Kaiser Community Paramedicine pilot program, in which paramedics and nurse practitioners proactively address the needs of frequent ED utilizers in the home in an effort to prevent them from returning to the ED. One of the findings was that some patients were not going to their follow-up appointments with their primary care providers after a home visit by paramedics, even if the appointment had been scheduled for them. Kaiser has now funded a "pilot within the pilot," with a control group and a research group, to study whether the use of vouchers for taxis will encourage patients to go to their appointments. Grant remarked that Kaiser is well suited for conducting such pilot studies because it has access to a vast amount of patient-level data over time within its system. With baseline data for individual patients, a transportation intervention can be introduced, use monitored, and outcomes assessed.

Noting that the paramedicine pilot is a very small study, Elmer asked about federal grant opportunities to fund a larger study to explore whether providing transportation does improve health outcomes. Yaffee suggested approaching the local metropolitan planning organization and becoming involved in its FTA Section 5310 process. Stock reiterated that FTA has demonstration grants, and has 5 years' worth of funding in the Fixing America's Surface Transportation (FAST) Act for competitive programs, including the types of demonstrations being discussed. Vince Valdes, the associate administrator for research, demonstration, and innovation at FTA, mentioned the Mobility on Demand Sandbox, with $8 million to be awarded for mobility-on-demand public transportation demonstration projects.[10]

Marsha Regenstein, a professor of health policy at George Washington University, pointed out that one out of every six dollars spent in the United States is spent on goods and services associated with health care. Whether for-profit, nonprofit, or public, health care providers design services around their businesses, she continued. She cautioned against assuming that all health care providers actually want the people in their communities to come to their locations. Many health care systems have moved away from inner cities and other areas with large need because the desired populations are elsewhere, she observed. These desired populations are where the money is.

Moderator Hughes-Cromwick reminded participants of the examples presented earlier by Kell and others (see Chapter 4) on making a compelling case for a cost-effective return on transportation projects.

## Bridging Across Surveys

There was discussion among participants, including White, Cynamon, and Janet Lynott of the AARP Public Policy Institute, of the potential value of linking the National Household Travel Survey and the National Health Interview Survey and potentially others as well. Cynamon said that the new core questionnaire for the National Health Interview Survey will be about 40 minutes long and that other agencies have the opportunity to add questions that can change from year to year (for a fee, no more than 5 minutes on a particular topic, about 20 minutes total of additional questions). Ed Christopher, an independent consultant, agreed and suggested that one way to enhance the large national surveys discussed would be to add context from other surveys. For example, in the past the National Household Travel Survey has added land use characteristics to records without making the survey questionnaire longer. If agencies could link or cross-tag their major surveys, it could provide rich information, he said. White cautioned that matching across data is not necessarily easy to do. For example, the U.S. Postal Service has a master registry of addresses that is not available to other statistical agencies. It may be possible to know the address of someone who has completed the National Household Travel Survey, but there could be a different person at the same address who completed the National Health Interview Survey. Cynamon responded that it would not have to be a direct match to the same household. Grant suggested using some type of common geographic identifier for linkage that is above the individual level,

[10] Applications closed on July 5, 2016. See https://www.transit.dot.gov/research-innovation/mobility-demand-mod-sandbox-program.html (accessed August 4, 2016).

such as the county level. This could allow the user to aggregate data around a common point across different surveys.

### Engaging Safety Net Hospitals

A participant from America's Essential Hospitals said that safety net hospitals deal with these issues on a day-to-day basis and are recognizing the excessive costs in ED visits. They are also recognizing the problem that a lack of transportation poses in large population health management. She encouraged participants to reach out to the safety net hospitals in their areas as partners in addressing transportation issues.

# 7

# Connecting Patients to Transportation: Incentives and Return on Investment

The last panel of the workshop included several examples of current solutions for connecting patients to transportation. Valerie Lefler, the president and chief executive officer of Liberty Mobility Now, Inc., described Liberty Connect and Liberty Now, two customer-based transportation solutions that work together to facilitate trips. Alex Page, the lead transportation planner for Ride Connection in Portland, Oregon, discussed a dialysis transportation pilot project as an example of linking accessible, responsive transportation with individual and community needs. David Riley, the director of the Veterans Transportation Program at the U.S. Department of Veterans Affairs (VA), provided an overview of the Veterans Health Administration (VHA) travel authorities, which allow for transportation for the purposes of examination, treatment, or care.

The presentations were followed by comments from discussants Virginia Dize, the co-director of the National Aging and Disability Transportation Center at the National Association of Area Agencies on Aging (n4a); Ed Christopher, an independent consultant formerly with the Federal Highway Administration; and Joseph Cronin, the John R. Kerr Research Chair in Marketing in the Department of Marketing, and co-director of the Marketing Institute at the College of Business at Florida State University. The session was moderated by Marsha Regenstein, a professor in the Department of Health Policy at George Washington University. (Highlights are presented in Box 7-1.)

**BOX 7-1**
**Highlights and Main Points Made by Individual Speakers and Participants[a]**

- Inclusive planning is a key element of success. It is important to directly engage the people who will be served by community transportation in the planning process and to understand what their specific needs are. (Dize, Lefler, Page, Riley)
- Education can improve transportation. Transportation providers might not understand what accommodations the patient needs; health care providers often do not know the transportation options available and therefore cannot advocate for patients; and patients are often unaware of or do not understand how to use the transportation that is available in the community. (Dize, Page)
- Different stakeholders view return on investment differently, depending on their individual goals. (Christopher, Lefler)
- Cross-sector collaboration will be aided by developing a shared vocabulary and shared metrics. (Cronin, Riley)
- There is an immediate need to make the business case that investing in transportation to care is of economic value, and there is also a need for longer-term research that demonstrates improvement in quality of life and the impacts of prevention. (Riley)

[a] This list is the rapporteurs' summary of the main points made by individual speakers and participants (noted in parentheses) and does not reflect any consensus among workshop participants or endorsement by the National Academies of Sciences, Engineering, and Medicine.

## LIBERTY

During the time that Lefler was studying public transportation in the state of Nebraska, there were 58 Federal Transit Authority (FTA) Section 5311 rural public transit providers and almost 90 FTA Section 5310 (seniors and individuals with disabilities) public transportation providers, and numerous challenges to mobility were identified. There were some counties with no transit service at all, Lefler said. There were county/city jurisdictional barriers and challenges with coordinating schedules and pricing. Adding vehicles to increase capacity could take up to 2 years, she noted. There was limited night and weekend service and few options for paratransit service, and urban taxis were traveling to communities 200 to 300 miles away to provide service (charging regular taxi rates). Research also showed that there was a limited awareness of transit service.

Lefler and her colleagues sought to create a customer-based transportation solution that would optimize existing resources, use community-based staffing, plug in mobility options where needed, and be affordable and quick to implement. The technology would need to be able to function under conditions found in rural communities (e.g., low Internet connection bandwidth) and to work on any technology platform (e.g., iOS, Android, PC, etc.). They ultimately developed two solutions, Liberty Connect and Liberty Now.[1] Liberty Connect uses a Software as a Service model that connects customers, transit agencies, and human service, medical, and care agencies. Liberty Now is an advanced centralized call center staffed by mobility managers using intelligent transportation systems.

## Liberty Connect

Liberty Connect is designed for agencies providing transportation service under FTA Section 5311 and 5310 programs and also for nonprofits. Liberty Connect includes a caregiver portal, a bus driver mobile application, and a mobile application for passengers, all connected to a transit dispatcher platform (see Figure 7-1).

The transit dispatcher dashboard shows the geographic information system (GIS) location of all vehicles currently in service. The dashboard also shows if a vehicle needs maintenance, based on a daily inspection checklist. Lefler emphasized that she and her team sought to make the platform intuitive and straightforward to use. All of the transportation requests, whether from the caregiver portal, the passenger mobile application, or the local call-in dispatcher, go into a pending request list. The transportation dispatcher at the local agency maintains control of the system. There is also a reporting function, including driver logs by day, week, month, and quarter; revenue miles; non-revenue miles; deadhead time (driving without a passenger); and passengers.

The caregiver portal allows the agencies (e.g., hospitals, doctors' offices, nursing homes, assisted living facilities, community action agencies, etc.) to book transportation and track rides. The portal also provides flexible billing options and reporting and helps reduce stress on the agency and improve client transportation. The provider's office can see who is coming for their appointments and where they are. The portal also allows the office to contact the driver when the patient is ready to be picked up to go home.

The bus driver mobile application works on iOS and Android mobile

[1] Integrated Global Dimensions is the parent company that developed Liberty. Funding for research and development has come from the U.S. Department of Transportation, the Federal Transit Administration, and the Small Business Administration. The Texas Department of Transportation, NMotion, and Invest Nebraska have provided venture capital support. For more information see http://thisisliberty.com (accessed August 4, 2016).

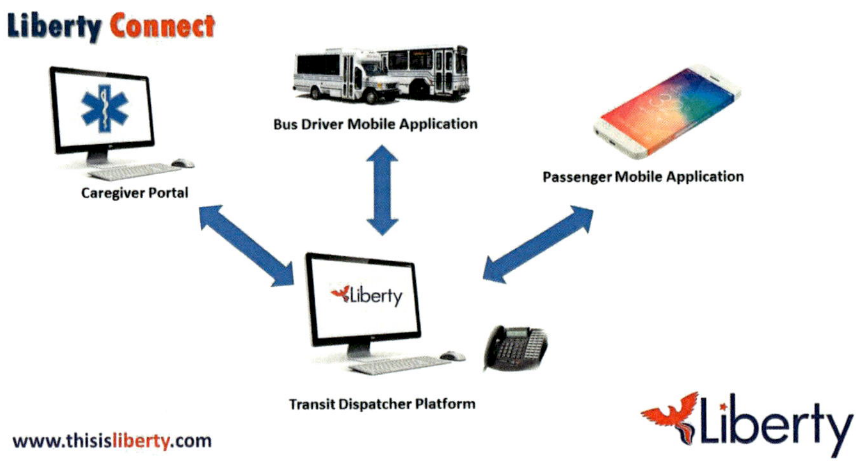


**FIGURE 7-1** Liberty Connect infrastructure.
SOURCE: Lefler presentation, June 7, 2016.

platforms, and it allows drivers to see details about their trips for the day. Drivers can enter updates at each step of the trip (e.g., passenger picked up, trip completed), and GIS data are pulled every 3 seconds, providing the place and time of each event that is happening. These data provide useful customer service information for reporting purposes, Lefler noted. They also allow for update notifications to the individuals using the passenger mobile application.

The passenger mobile application is very simple, Lefler said, comparing it to the applications used by Uber or Lyft. Passengers can see their upcoming trips and receive notifications.

Liberty Connect was launched in June 2016 and is currently being used in Scotts Bluff, Nebraska. Lefler said that it will be expanded to several new sites in the coming months, and additional functions will be added (e.g., credit card payment processing, customer satisfaction ratings, automated ticket tracking).

### Liberty Now

Liberty Now is designed for nonemergency medical transportation (NEMT), nonmedical transportation, statewide and regional mobility management, and community hospital access to care centers. It is a centralized call center with dedicated mobility managers who search for the best solution for each individual, including public transit options, nonprofit service agencies, Liberty drivers, taxis, Uber or Lyft, volunteer drivers, and family members. Local Liberty mobility managers are hired from the community, so they know the micro-cultures and the roads, Lefler said, and Liberty drivers are independent contractors. Taking lessons from the railroads and the shipping and logistics industries, Lefler and colleagues designed intelligent transportation systems to collect and use data to track high-priority, high-vulnerability transports (e.g., dialysis patients, individuals in the late stages of Alzheimer's disease) to make sure they arrive where and when needed. There is sophisticated trip scheduling technology and automated booking and routing. The emphasis is on using data to monitor customer service, identify gaps and opportunities, and improve passenger, caregiver, provider, and driver satisfaction.

Local Liberty mobility managers conduct local driver recruitment, screening, and training; follow up on customer service interventions if concerns are reported; and provide customer service and education. They gather constant business intelligence about mobility options. The Mobility Champions Circle includes local individuals and consumer advocates who work together to keep everyone apprised of any changes in options (e.g., rates, routes, and schedules of local public transportation agencies, which change frequently). Mobility managers also serve as emergency drivers of last resort. Lefler added that there is a launch team available to assist the Local Liberty mobility managers over the first 90 days, including a logistics specialist, a community engagement specialist, and a marketing strategist.

Liberty drivers are members of the local community, and they set their hours and service area on a weekly basis. Lefler added that the majority of trips are prescheduled. Customer service training, cardiopulmonary resuscitation, first aid, and lap belt training are required. Liberty drivers use their personal vehicles, which must be clean and well maintained, and are subject to random vehicle inspections. Drivers must also to pass a strict background check, including fingerprinting, driver's license check, and vehicle title inspection. Lefler said that 80 percent of the ride fare stays in the community, paid to the local driver (the other 20 percent pays for Liberty infrastructure). This is very important in rural economic regions where there are very few part-time jobs, she said.

The two solutions now work together, and the Liberty Now automated or manual trip request appears in the Liberty Connect transit manager's dispatch log, Lefler said in conclusion.

## RIDE CONNECTION

Ride Connection is a nonprofit transportation provider in the Portland, Oregon, region that helps link accessible, responsive transportation with individual and community needs, Page said. The vision is to create independence and community connectors through travel options. Ride Connection services include demand response (eg., curb-to-curb, door-to-door, door-through-door) using volunteer and paid drivers; community connectors (i.e., first-mile/last-mile connectors); shopping shuttles for seniors; travel training; and fare relief. Ride Connection also partners with more than 30 organizations in the Portland metropolitan area, providing resources such as driver training (e.g., lift operation, blood-borne pathogen training) and providing vehicles owned by Ride Connection.

### Dahlia Dialysis Transportation Pilot

Page described the Dahlia Dialysis Transportation Pilot project as an example of a Ride Connection program. The project was funded by the Administration for Community Living, in partnership with the Community Transportation Association of America, Easterseals, and the n4a. The planning process was very inclusive, involving stakeholders, an advisory committee, focus groups, one-on-one interviews, caregiver surveys, patient surveys, a workshop, and workgroups. Months were spent researching the needs of the community, the clinics, and the transportation providers. Page said that dialysis patients are frequently asked to fill out surveys, and a common complaint is that they never hear back on the results of the survey. As part of this project, patients and clinic workers were provided with feedback throughout the process, he said. Patients and providers identified a variety of barriers to patient transport to and from dialysis, including the frequency of visits, the costs, scheduling, the special care needed, and the inflexibility of transportation providers.

Several community resource ideas emerged out of the planning process, Page said, all of them focused on education and volunteer recruitment. It was found that there was a lack of understanding among the transportation providers and the public of what dialysis is and what accommodations patients might need. For example, drivers had no idea that patients were in discomfort or pain and that they might be taking speed bumps too quickly for a patient's comfort. Clinics did not understand the transportation options available to them. They knew them by name and phone number, but they were not advocates for the patients. To deal with these issues, the project included education for the transportation providers (i.e., classroom and online training, a video, patient dialogue) and outreach to the clinics. Page shared a clip from a video that is part of a full-day training program.[2] The training has been very effective, he said, adding that some

[2] The video is available at https://rideconnection.org/services/additional-programs/dahlia (accessed August 4, 2016).

transportation providers are giving their employees a small hourly wage increase to incentivize participation in the training.

From the inclusive planning process, Ride Connection implemented a pilot project with elements and changes designed to improve the effectiveness of transportation for dialysis patients. Elements of the pilot included, for example, a dedicated dispatcher, collaboration with partners, no costs to patients, allowing shared rides, training, and constant communication. A critical aspect of the pilot, Page said, is a quarterly assessment of the level of service for the patients.

Page reviewed the program costs, noting that the goal is not to be the cheapest ride, but to be the most appropriate ride for a dialysis patient. The average trip costs $16.32, which he suggested is low compared to other paratransit options. He said that the cost per ride has been increasing in recent months as the number of paid driver hours needed has increased. At the start, the project relied heavily on volunteer hours, but the number of volunteer hours has decreased over time, due in part to overworking of volunteers, slow recruitment, and having only one volunteer coordinator.

The ultimate goal is improved patient outcomes, and Page highlighted several key outcomes thus far. The majority of actual dialysis times more closely match the prescription times; missed appointments have decreased significantly; and patient health and quality of life have improved. Page acknowledged that quality of life is very difficult to assess, and the pilot relies on qualitative evidence from surveys. Patients have reported that the transportation project has improved their lives and that their stress is reduced by not having to worry about transportation.

Meanwhile, clinics are spending less time dealing with transportation issues, they have a better understanding of the transportation options for dialysis patients, and they are better advocates for their patients. All of this leads to saved time and money, Page said.

In closing, Page emphasized that collaboration is required for success and said that the educational component alone can help improve transportation. He cautioned against putting too much emphasis on financial return on investment; the focus should instead be a more holistic one, taking into account shared investments and shared values. Each stakeholder has different immediate needs, but all can agree to rally around better patient health outcomes. Going forward, Ride Connection is looking to replicate the dialysis transportation model with other chronic conditions and care facilities.

## VETERANS TRANSPORTATION PROGRAM

The Veterans Transportation Program includes the Beneficiary Travel program, the Veterans Transportation Service, and the Highly Rural Transportation Grants program. Riley focused his remarks on the VHA travel authorities that allow for transportation for the purposes of examination, treatment, or care.

The Beneficiary Travel program assists eligible veterans and other beneficiaries by offsetting the cost of their travel to VA and VA-authorized health care. Low-income and service-connected veterans are eligible for reimbursement for mileage or for third-party transportation. The Beneficiary Travel program costs were about $850 million in fiscal year 2015, and projected costs for fiscal year 2017 are about $924 million. A program of this size and visibility is frequently audited, and Riley said that errors in mileage reimbursement claim payments do occur. About 55 percent of enrolled veterans at the VA meet eligibility requirements for beneficiary travel. For the other 45 percent, the Veterans Transportation Service allows VA facilities to hire mobility managers, drivers, and ride schedulers as well as to purchase Americans with Disabilities Act (ADA)–compliant vehicles to transport beneficiaries to their health care appointments. However, Riley said, even with these two transportation authorities, there is a gap in coverage.

The Veterans Transportation Service was launched in 2010 with four sites, and today there are more than 100 sites participating (roughly two-thirds of the VA medical centers). This is not a mandatory program, Riley said, and uptake has required using metrics to convince leadership at VA hospitals that providing transportation is a good business decision.

One challenge is to demonstrate the sustainability of the Veterans Transportation Program. Although a few medical center directors will support anything that improves access, most need to see a benefit to their bottom line. If the program cannot pay for itself, Riley explained, directors will spend that money on other medical services and are likely to see transportation as a luxury. Since the inception of the Veterans Transportation Program, the program has collected data on trips and service miles; there have been more than 1 million trips, totaling more than 25 million service miles. One way to demonstrate value is to show how the Veterans Transportation Program offset costs from the $850 million Beneficiary Travel program. Costs are offset by intercepting some of the rides that would otherwise go to community providers. The mobility manager for the Veterans Transportation Program can compare the cost of using the set rate contract (for a third-party provider of a special mode of transportation) with the cost of using the VA's own Veterans Transportation Program services. In addition, because the Veterans Transportation Program can transport more than one beneficiary at a time (e.g., in ADA-compliant vans), it is possible to also include veterans who are not beneficiary travel–eligible and transport them at the same time.

Another way to show value is to demonstrate a reduction in missed opportunities (e.g., missed appointments, cancellations made too late to schedule another beneficiary in that time slot). Because the VHA has patient data from over the long term, it is able to demonstrate that transportation provided in a targeted manner can reduce missed opportunities. On an aggregate level, there has been about a 1 percent decrease in missed opportunities since the time before the implementation of the transportation program. The improvement was not uniform across facilities, Riley said, suggesting that it would be worthwhile to investigate why there is substantial improvement at some facilities and negative results at others. On an individual level, patients with high missed opportunity rates may be more likely to miss appointments because of transportation difficulties than patients with low missed opportunity rates, and perhaps the transportation program should be targeted at them.

Patient satisfaction is also used as a metric, and internal controls are used to demonstrate that the payments made are correct and that the services offered are for the appropriate population.

In closing, Riley highlighted several future needs. A longitudinal study is needed, he said, that includes specific subpopulations and focuses on quality of life and missed opportunities. Metrics are needed that include the degree of difficulty of the transport (e.g., rurality, traveler's health condition, the need for enabling services). Riley suggested that the metrics should take into account the intended approach (i.e., access or cost offset). He also suggested that targeted resources are needed for sites focusing on special populations (e.g., the homeless and those with spinal cord injuries who are on dialysis or who have mental health issues). It is important to be able to demonstrate that these costly special populations are being served by the Veterans Transportation Service and that transporting them to care is saving money for the health care system in the long run. Transportation for patient flow is a potentially useful metric to consider (e.g., on-demand transport for discharged patients to reduce additional bed days of care). There is also a need for transportation for mental health 14-day follow-up visits, and Riley said that several VHA sites have shown that when transportation is provided, patients will come in for their follow-up appointments.

## DISCUSSION

Following the presentations, participants continued the discussion of inclusive planning. Participants also expressed a range of opinions on how best to demonstrate the return on investment in health-related transportation in order to ensure the sustainability of programs, including the merits of sound economic arguments versus ethical and social arguments.

### Inclusive Planning

The n4a has long had an interest in transportation, and its member Area Agencies on Aging around the country also consider transportation to be among their top priorities, Dize said. The National Aging and Disability Transportation Center is a partnership between n4a and Easterseals and is one of three federal transportation technical assistance centers funded by FTA. The center focuses on accessibility of transportation for older adults, people with disabilities of all ages, and family caregivers.

It is critically important, Dize emphasized, that individuals have access to information about the transportation that is available in their communities. The National Aging and Disability Transportation Center has a partnership with the Eldercare Locator, which provides information to older adults and caregivers about a wide variety of issues and resources. Transportation is the number one reason that people call the Eldercare Locator, Dize said, ranking above Social Security, Medicare, Medicaid, and other critical concerns. Between October 2015 and March 2016, the Eldercare Locator handled more than 16,000 calls on transportation issues, the majority of which were from older people who desperately needed a ride to medical services, Dize said.

It is also critically important to talk directly with the people who will be served by community transportation about what their needs are, Dize continued. Another way in which n4a is involved in transportation is through the Inclusive Coordinated Transportation Partnership Project, which is funded by the Administration for Community Living, and is being carried out in partnership with the Community Transportation Association of America and Easterseals. The project focuses on engaging older adults and people with disabilities in community transportation service planning. Dize said that Ride Connection (discussed above by Page) is one of the grantees. When considering return on investment, Dize said, it important to ensure that the investment being made is the "right" investment—that it is actually supporting the needs of people who are living in the community.

Page agreed and reiterated that the Dahlia Dialysis Transportation Pilot project focuses on providing the most appropriate ride, which is not necessarily the least expensive ride. Anyone whom Ride Connection partners with to provide rides receives training to ensure the highest levelof customer service. Page said he considers Ride Connection more as an advocate for the customer than a transportation provider. He added that the inclusive planning pilot project allowed Ride Connection to test its outreach capabilities and its ability to collaborate with multiple stakeholders and different interests and to work toward defining the shared value in the shared investment.

Lefler agreed with the importance of establishing shared goals at the start of a partnership and defining the population being served and the desired outcomes. Working with the customer is the best way to determine what the goals are. Clearly defined goals are needed for monitoring progress on a regular basis and also for transparency. In establishing Liberty, eight focus groups were held to better understand the ecosystem in each environment. Participants included farmers, persons older than age 85, drivers, veterans, and other stakeholders. What is right in one community may be different from what is right in another community, Lefler said. Riley added that the Veterans Transportation Service also engages stakeholders in transportation to help guide the program.

### Social Versus Economic Arguments in Demonstrating the Returns to Health from Investments in Transportation

There is stiff competition for limited transportation resources, Ed Christopher said, and Congress requires justification for the spending of public money to ensure that the money spent achieves a positive return. In assessing return on investment, Christopher said, it is important to carefully consider the questions that need to be answered as well as the metrics needed to answer them. He observed that return on investment is viewed differently by different stakeholders. For transportation access to care, he said, the questions revolve around whether the efforts are making people healthier.

Lefler noted that return on investment is difficult to ascertain in health care because it depends on illness, age, income level, and other factors of the many individuals involved. The ultimate question is whether quality of life is being improved. One of Liberty's goals is to expand the ecosystem of transportation options. While the primary focus is on providing options to get to medical care, individuals might also find suitable options for visiting loved ones, for example, or for when driving themselves might not be a safe option for them. When making the business case to policy makers and legislators, the task is to show how transportation can be provided in the most efficient way possible. She agreed with Christopher that justifying the expense depends on the goals of the stakeholders.

Transportation is essential to quality of life, Riley agreed. He suggested that a long-term study using patient data and a quality-of-life scale could demonstrate the value of transportation, especially if that transportation was not limited to transport to medical care. From a business perspective, return on investment could be demonstrated by measuring the impact of transportation in those areas of health care that generate high costs. For example, can access to transportation eliminate the need to move an individual into a nursing home? Does access to transportation reduce the need for an extended inpatient hospital stay when discharge is possible? This is a piecemeal approach, he acknowledged, but many such examples could make the case for investing in transportation.

Page emphasized that access to care is an equity issue as well and that people should not be denied health care because they cannot get to it. He suggested that there is a moral argument to be made as well, when justifying programs to Congress. Another participant agreed that there is a moral argument to be made for transportation to care, but said that it is economics that make the case for investment and that perhaps there is a moral imperative to make the economic case on behalf of those who are poor, marginalized, and disempowered.

Cronin highlighted the need for new and innovative cross-discipline research and stressed the need to "speak the language" of those you are trying to convince. He described some of his early work on return-on-investment calculations for medically related transportation services. One approach is to calculate cost avoidance (as a result of, for example, reduced ED visits, hospitalizations, or missed days of work). He said that much of the work at that time was based on assumptions about relationships between transportation and care (e.g., how many trips to care might correlate with avoidance of a 1-day in-hospital stay). He agreed that medical trips are about quality of life improvement, but he added that those controlling the funding (i.e., the tax dollars) want to show that they are generating a financial return. He encouraged participants to identify the economic benefits of getting people to care. These benefits range from eliminating missed appointments to keeping people out of the hospital. It is not making a profit, he emphasized—it is avoiding a cost, which can be a significant benefit for many businesses. Cronin encouraged participants from the health care field to engage business schools, which he said are willing to help.

A participant concurred with the need for a real collaboration between the transportation side and the health side. He acknowledged the challenges, including the fact that many in the health care field do not have an adequate understanding of the essential role of transportation assistance in getting people to care. He also agreed with the need to make a sound economic argument, but he suggested that the phrase "return on investment" is not ideal for this discussion. He noted the general aversion to viewing transportation to health care as a business model, but he asserted that there are financial savings to be realized when, for example, a child with asthma is well controlled in the primary care setting. One can compare the primary care visit and medication costs spent to the ED and hospitalizations avoided and demonstrate the return on investment.

Lefler agreed with the concept of demonstrating returns in terms of cost savings. She cited the example of using a Liberty driver who lives in the community versus calling an urban taxi service to travel to a rural community. Page suggested thinking in terms of risk mitigation.

Riley also highlighted the need for a shared vocabulary and shared metrics that address concrete issues (i.e., established costs that can be intercepted or prevented). He called for both short- and long-term planning and suggested that there is an immediate need to demonstrate the business case to Congress and health and transportation leadership, to show them that investing in transportation to care is of value to them. Riley added that there is also the need for a long-term body of research that demonstrates improvement in quality of life and the impacts of prevention.

# 8

# Reflections on the Workshop

## SPONSOR PERSPECTIVE

In the final session of the workshop, Vince Valdes, the associate administrator for research, demonstration, and innovation at the Federal Transit Administration (FTA) in the U.S. Department of Transportation, reflected on the workshop on behalf of the sponsor organization. There has always been a connection between transportation and health care, he said. This workshop at the National Academies of Sciences, Engineering, and Medicine (the National Academies) has helped to bring it to the forefront. This conversation needs to continue, he said, and he shared his perspective on next steps for moving forward. In particular, he suggested several actions that will be important to success:

- **Establish a shared value system focused on making people's lives better.** In establishing those basic shared values, Valdes said, it will be important to remember that this is an endeavor for people. It is person-centric, traveler-centric, and patient-centric. In providing better health care and providing better transportation to health care, people are providing the aspects that make for a better quality of life.
- **Develop a common language.** Valdes observed that even at the workshop there were differences among the panelists in terms of the language they use and the stakeholders they serve.
- **Define common metrics.** It is important to start measuring those factors in people's lives that make for better living overall, Valdes said, including the quality of life and the quality of health care. It

will also be important to agree on common metrics and measures of success and to be able to demonstrate that the people who are being served are getting better service, are satisfied with the service, and are experiencing a better quality of life.

- **Continue to pilot new models of providing transportation services to enhance life.** From the FTA perspective, Valdes said, it is important to continue to pilot new and exciting ways of providing transportation services for different sectors and client bases and to pilot these opportunities through partnerships. Rides to Wellness is based on the mobility-on-demand model, which has broader goals than just wellness, Valdes said. It is really "rides to life," he said, and he suggested that a ride should be a ride, whether to recreation, to health care, or to a job. People need transportation; it is at once a commodity, a utility, and a social service, he said. Through the Mobility on Demand demonstration program, FTA is looking for best practices and innovative pilots of user-centric approaches to providing different aspects of service for people who need it.
- **Reach out across federal agencies to get perspectives on the user base for public transportation.** It will be important going forward, Valdes said, to continue relationships across sectors and to reach out across the federal space to help bring the perspectives of the diverse user base to public transportation.

## PARTICIPANT PERSPECTIVES

Ysela Llort called on participants to share their final observations. Many took the opportunity to highlight available resources and opportunities. Participants also offered additional thoughts on next steps.

### General Comments

A webcast participant agreed with the need for uniform definitions and emphasized the importance of focusing on data that can make the case to funding agencies. Information such as lost revenues due to lack of transportation is useful. Webcast viewer Suzanne O'Neill commented that measuring how transportation is able to keep people living independently is important because it relates to quality of life. Better efforts are also needed to match costs and benefits, she added. It will not possible to increase resources for transportation if the local communities are being asked to pay for the costs, while the benefits are occurring at the state or federal levels or going to a for-profit dialysis center, for example. The participant stressed that those at the federal level need to have the ability to make the best decisions for resources and mobility. The current system, in which the program is left trying to shift costs to others, is not sustainable.

Webcast participant Charlotte Frye asked why it appears to fall to FTA to meet mobility needs, while the Federal Highway Administration (FHWA) focuses on moving vehicles. In other words, why is the connection to health care directed to FTA, when it should be a larger objective for all of the U.S. Department of Transportation (DOT)? Valdes responded that FHWA is as committed to mobility as FTA and other stakeholders. As an example of its activities, he said that FHWA is currently funding the Accessible Transportation Technology Research Initiative, an initiative to facilitate mobility for people with disabilities. U.S. DOT is unified in its commitment to a multimodal approach to transportation.

## Resources and Opportunities

Valerie Lefler told participants that $377 million in research funding will be awarded through the University Transportation Center program grant competition out of the Office of the Assistant Secretary for Research and Technology. The focus of the funded research over the next 5 years will be ways to improve the mobility of people and goods. She encouraged participants to watch the website for the forthcoming announcement of the national, regional, and tier 1 University Transportation Centers.[1] The research dollars are there, she said, and the office will be looking for topics to study. Valdes added that the Transit Cooperative Research Program and the Highway Cooperative Research Program, both administered by the Transportation Research Board (TRB), are soliciting ideas for research.[2]

Karen White informed participants that FTA has three technical assistance centers available to help them. The National Rural Transit Assistance Program collects, disseminates, and aids best practices for rural transportation. The National Aging and Disability Transportation Center assists Section 5310 program recipients in providing services for older adults and people with disabilities. The National Center for Mobility Management aids and provides technical assistance with regard to mobility management for all sectors of the transportation industry.[3]

Llort reminded participants that some of the surveys discussed at the workshop are seeking input on revisions and encouraged them to take the opportunity to comment (specifically, the 2018 redesign of the National Health Interview Survey discussed by Marcie Cynamon).[4]

Ed Christopher encouraged participants to sign up for the listserv of the TRB Health and Transportation Subcommittee, which is focusing

[1] See http://www.rita.dot.gov/utc (accessed August 4, 2016).

[2] See http://www.trb.org/AboutTRB/AboutCooperativeResearchPrograms.aspx (accessed August 4, 2016).

[3] See http://nationalrtap.org, http://www.nadtc.org, and http://nationalcenterformobilitymanagement.org (all accessed August 4, 2016).

[4] See Chapter 6.

on health and transportation issues broadly (i.e., not limited to access to care).[5] He also alerted participants to the TRB 2016 John and Jane Public Competition, which is seeking best practices in communicating the connection between transportation and public health to the average citizen on the street.[6]

### Final Thoughts to Inform Future Work

Oscar Gomez highlighted the need for more awareness, observing that much has been done, and is currently being done, but many working on the health care side are not aware of these activities. He offered to try to document the current partnerships and identify key stakeholders on the transportation side and the health care side as well as some potential partners from other sectors (e.g., foundations).

Martin Ornelas suggested that a formal assessment of all the current federal agencies involved in transit would also be highly valuable. Kate Lawson suggested the need for a clearinghouse of information about developing partnerships, such as navigating nondisclosure agreements, accessing data within the parameters of the Health Insurance Portability and Accountability Act, and working with institutional review boards.

Jana Lynott said that many good research ideas were presented at the workshop and suggested that a research proposal be developed that spans both the transportation sector and the health sector for submission to the TRB Transit Cooperative Research Program and the Health and Medicine Division of the National Academies. Llort suggested that proposals for both short-term and longer-term type of activities would be of interest.

Steve Yaffe suggested convening a planning committee that can refine the objectives for developing a common dataset. The next step would be to invite experts in the data discussed at the workshop to conduct a mapping project to draw the links of commonality across sectors and consider how and whether it will be possible to come together on the common objectives.

This has to be a continuing dialogue if the community is indeed committed to making a change and to improving that which it values, which is human life and wellness, Llort concluded.

[5] See http://www.trbhealth.org (accessed August 4, 2016).

[6] For more information, see https://sites.google.com/site/trbcommitteeada60/jjpcompetition/2016-communicating-the-connection-transportation-and-public-health (accessed August 4, 2016).

# A

# References

Grant, R., A. Ramgoolam, R. Betz, L. Ruttner, and J. J. Green. 2010. Challenges to accessing pediatric health care in the Mississippi Delta: A survey of emergency department patients seeking nonemergency care. *Journal of Primary Care and Community Health* 1(3):152–157.

Health Outreach Partners. 2014. *Overcoming obstacles to health care: Transportation models that work.* http://outreach-partners.org/2014/06/04/overcoming-obstacles-to-health-care-transportation-models-that-work (accessed October 25, 2016).

McClintock, M. K., W. Dale, E. O. Laumann, and L. Waite. 2016. Empirical redefinition of comprehensive health and well-being in the older adults of the United States. *Proceedings of the National Academy of Sciences of the United States of America* 113(22):E3071–E3080.

Myers, A. 2015. Non-Emergency Medical Transportation: A Vital Lifeline For A Healthy Community. National Conference on State Legislatures. http://www.ncsl.org/research/transportation/non-emergency-medical-transportation-a-vital-lifeline-for-a-healthy-community.aspx (accessed August 31, 2016).

NASEM (National Academies of Sciences, Engineering, and Medicine.) 2016. *Metrics That Matter for Population Health Action: Workshop Summary.* Washington, DC: The National Academies Press.

Stiefel, M. C., C. L. Riley, B. Roy, R. Ramaswamy, and S. Stout. 2016. *100 Million Healthier Lives Measurement System: Progress to Date.* 100 Million Healthier Lives Metrics Development Team Report. Cambridge, MA: Institute for Healthcare Improvement. http://www.100mlives.org/measure (accessed August 4, 2016).

TRB (Transportation Research Board). 2016. *TRB Special Report 319: Between Public and Private Mobility: Examining the Rise of Technology-Enabled Transportation Services.* Washington, DC: Transportation Research Board.

# B

# Workshop Agenda

**Health and Medicine Division and Transportation Research Board**

**Exploring Data and Metrics of Value at the Intersection of Health Care and Transportation: A Workshop**
**June 6–7, 2016**

Location: National Academy of Sciences Building, 2101 Constitution Avenue NW, Washington, DC; Room 125

**DRAFT WORKSHOP OBJECTIVES:**

1. To showcase models of transportation services that facilitate individuals' access to health care providers.
2. To discuss data sources, information technology obstacles and solutions from and across the health care and transportation perspectives.
3. To explore opportunities to ascertain the value realized by transportation providers, health systems, and funders/payers if providing transportation services results in improved health outcomes.

**June 6, 2016**

8:15 am **Welcome and overview of the day**

*Ysela Llort, former director, Miami-Dade Transit; planning committee chair*

*Neil Pedersen, executive director, Transportation Research Board (TRB), National Academies of Sciences, Engineering, and Medicine*

*Clyde Behney, executive director, Health and Medicine Division, National Academies of Sciences, Engineering, and Medicine*

8:40 am **Setting the context: FTA-supported efforts**

*Carolyn Flowers, acting administrator, Federal Transit Administration (FTA), U.S. Department of Transportation (DOT) (Welcome)*

*Bruce Robinson, acting associate administrator for program management, FTA (Overview of FTA's Rides to Wellness initiative)*

*Oscar Gomez, chief executive officer, Health Outreach Partners (Overview of the Rides to Wellness Community Scan)*

9:15 am **Setting the context: Other relevant efforts in the field**

*Heidi Guenin, senior associate, GridWorks, Portland, Oregon*

9:30 am **Q&A/discussion**

*Discussants: Flora Castillo, vice president of community and strategic engagement, UnitedHealthcare; Heather MacLeod, assistant director, Physical Infrastructure, Seattle Field Office, U.S. Government Accountability Office; Judy Shanley, vice president, Education and Youth Transition at Easterseals, Inc. (partner in National Center for Mobility Management); Julie Bershadsky, senior research specialist, Human Services Research Institute*

10:10 am **Panel I: Examples of cross-sector collaboration to provide transportation services in urban settings (10 minutes/presenter)**

*Moderator: Nigel Wilson, professor, Civil and Environmental Engineering, Massachusetts Institute of Technology; planning committee member*

*Ann Lundy, vice president, Care Management, Health Care Service Corporation (by WebEx)*

*Perry Meadows, medical director, Government Programs, Geisinger Health Plan*

*Yahaira Graxirena, transportation planner, Central Massachusetts, Regional Planning Commission*

*Xavier Arinez, chief operating officer, Family Health Center of Worcester, Massachusetts*

*Mary Blumberg, program manager, Strategic Planning and Development, Atlanta Regional Commission*

*Katherine Kortum, study director,* Between Public and Private Mobility, *TRB*

11:15 am **Q&A/discussion with panel I**

*Discussants: Jana Lynott, senior strategic policy advisor, AARP; J. Barry Barker, executive director, Transit Authority of River City, Louisville, Kentucky; Art Guzzetti, vice president–policy, American Public Transit Association (APTA); Valerie Lefler, president and chief executive officer, Liberty Mobility Now, Inc.*

12:00 pm **Lunch**

1:00 pm **Panel II: Examples of cross-sector collaboration to provide transportation services in rural/small urban/ suburban settings**

*Moderator: Rich Garrity, senior associate, RLS & Associates; planning committee member*

*Judith Kell, hub operations manager, Pathways to Better Health of the Lakeshore, Mercy Health, Muskegon, Michigan*

*David Faldmo, medical director, Siouxland Community Health Center, Sioux City, Iowa*

*Suzanne Alewine, executive director, Missouri Rural Health Association*

*Dennis Johnson, executive vice president, Policy and Advocacy, Children's Health Fund*

1:45 pm **Q&A/discussion with panel II**

*Discussants: Charles Carr, director, Intermodal Planning, Mississippi Department of Transportation; Amy Conrick, assistant director, Community Transportation Association of America (CTAA); Robin Phillips, executive director, National Rural Transit Assistance Program; Marianne Stock, division chief, Rural and Targeted Programs, FTA*

2:45 pm **Break**

3:00 pm **Breakouts (presentations of local data and analyses, followed by discussion)**

*Facilitator: Michelle Proser, director of research, National Association of Community Health Centers; planning committee member*

*Presentation: Linking Transportation, Health, and the Built Environment in Washington, DC—Anneta Arno, director, Office of Health Equity, Office of the Director, District of Columbia Department of Health; Raka Choudhury, citywide transportation planner, Progressive Transportation Services Administration, District (of Columbia) Department of Transportation (DDOT); Steve Strauss, deputy associate director, Progressive Transportation Services Administration, DDOT*

*Presentation: Efficient and Effective Provision of Mobility to Health Care—Steve Yaffe, transit services manager, Arlington, Virginia*

*Facilitator: Flora Castillo, vice president of community and strategic engagement, UnitedHealthcare*

*Presentation: Smart Transit for Health Care—Moumita Dasgupta, principal investigator, Department of Physics and Astronomy, Amherst College; Sarah Anderson, business development manager, Cambridge Systematics, Inc.*

*Presentation: Comparing Scheduled and Actual Transit Accessibility to Health Centers—Anson Stewart, Interdepartmental Transportation Program, Massachusetts Institute of Technology*

4:00 pm **Reconvene in plenary for reporting back from breakout groups**

*Ysela Llort, planning committee chair*

5:00 pm **Adjourn**

## June 7, 2016

8:15 am **Welcome to Day 2**
*Ysela Llort, planning committee chair*

8:30 am **Panel III: Explore data sources available at different levels of government and in the public and private sectors; addressing a range of barriers (e.g., privacy, technical, operational)**
*Moderators: Catherine T. Lawson, professor, associate professor, Geography and Planning, State University of New York at Albany, and Paul Hughes-Cromwick, co-director, Center for Sustainable Health Spending, Altarum Institute; planning committee members*

*Chris Barnett, co-director, Center for Applied Research and Environmental Systems, University of Missouri at Columbia (and Community Commons)*

*Roy Grant, consultant (formerly at Children's Health Fund)*

*Marcie Cynamon, director, Division of Health Interview Statistics, National Center for Health Statistics, Centers for Disease Control and Prevention*

*Kelsey Walter, director of National Core Indicators-Aging and Disabilities, National Association of States United for Aging and Disabilities*

*Karen White, director, Office of Statistical and Economic Analysis, Bureau of Transportation Statistics, U.S. DOT*

9:30 am **Q&A/discussion with Panel III**
*Steve Yaffe, transit services manager, Arlington County; David Riley, director, Veterans Transportation Program, U.S. Department of Veterans Affairs; Peter McNichol, chief, Quality Control, NEMT,*[1] *Department of Vermont Health Access*

[1] Nonemergency medical transportation.

10:15 am **Panel IV: Data and barriers continued; return on investment and incentives for greater effectiveness in connecting patients to transportation**

*Moderator: Marsha Regenstein, professor, Department of Health Policy, George Washington University Milken Institute School of Public Health; planning committee member*

*Valerie Lefler, president and chief executive officer, Liberty Mobility Now, Inc.*

*Alex Page, lead transportation planner, RideConnection, Portland, Oregon*

*David Riley, director, Veterans Transportation Program, U.S. Department of Veterans Affairs*

*Julia Resnick, program manager, Health Research and Educational Trust, American Hospital Association (not present at workshop)*

11:00 am **Q&A/discussion with Panel IV**

*Discussants: Virginia Dize, co-director, National Aging and Disability Transportation Center, National Association of Area Agencies on Aging, TRB accessibility committee; Ed Christopher, consultant (formerly, Federal Highway Administration); Joseph Cronin, John R. Kerr Research Chair in Marketing, Department of Marketing, and co-director of the Marketing Institute, College of Business, Florida State University*

11:45 am **Reflections on the workshop, next steps**

*Ysela Llort, planning committee chair*

*Vincent Valdes, associate administrator for research, demonstration, and innovation, FTA*

12:30 pm **Closing remarks and adjournment**

For more information, visit http://nationalacademies.org/hmd/activities/publichealth/transitandhealthcare.aspx.

# C

# Environmental Scan

**Submitted to:**
**Health and Medicine Division and Transportation Research Board**
**By: Heidi Guenin, A.I.C.P., M.P.H.**

This environmental scan was supported by the Federal Transit Administration (FTA) and commissioned by the Health and Medicine Division (HMD) and the Transportation Research Board (TRB), program divisions of the National Academies of Sciences, Engineering, and Medicine. Heidi Guenin conducted the interviews and wrote this report. Special thanks to Ross Peterson, Principal of GridWorks, for providing input and feedback on this report.

The views in this environmental scan do not reflect the views of FTA, HMD, or TRB. For more information, contact Heidi Guenin at (503) 841-7936 or heidi@groxie.com.

## CONTENTS

PURPOSE 103

BACKGROUND 103
Health, 106
Transportation, 110
Return on Investment, 110

INTERVIEW BACKGROUND 112

SUMMARY OF THEMES 113

INTERVIEW THEMES: CHALLENGES 114
Defining Return on Investment, 114
Funding and Basic Infrastructure, 117
Missing Information and Data, 118
Technology, 122
Geography, 123
NEMT Destination and Service Gaps, 125
Cross-Sector Collaboration, 126

INTERVIEW THEMES: SOLUTIONS AND OPPORTUNITIES 130
Grants, 130
Shared Learning, 130
Start Small and Go Slow, 131
Let Patients Tell the Story, 133
Take the Care to the Patients, 134
Customer Experience, 134
Sharing Resources, Increasing Revenue, 135
Sharing Data, Analyzing Solutions, 137

AVAILABLE INFORMATION 138
Existing National Data, 139
Existing Local or Program-Specific Data, 143

RESEARCH AND RESOURCES 146
Completed Reports, 146
Reports Under Way or Planned for the Future, 155
Tools and Resources, 157

INTERVIEWEES 160

## PURPOSE

This environmental scan was conducted to support the Health and Medicine Division and the Transportation Research Board workshop: Exploring Data and Metrics of Value at the Intersection of Health Care and Transportation.[1]

Transportation impacts health outcomes directly, especially through physical activity, safety, and air quality (see Figure C-1). Transportation also impacts access to health care directly, and through access to care, transportation also affects health care costs and health outcomes indirectly. The purpose of this scan is to examine if and how transportation and health care partners explore the return on investment of providing transportation to health care or health-related destinations. More than 70 individuals were interviewed about health care and transportation partnerships, relevant data, and the value proposition of providing transportation to health care and health-related destinations.

## BACKGROUND

Transportation is well understood to be a significant factor in health care access. There are many ways that individuals access health care and other health supportive services, including walking, bicycling, riding fixed-route transit (e.g., bus or subway), using a taxi cab or shared ride service, or calling an ambulance. While some individuals have financial, physical, and cultural access to these transportation options and more, others have few to no transportation options to help them access health care. As a direct result they may delay or miss preventive or primary care appointments, not make it for follow-up care, or may be unable to fill prescriptions or access other health supports.

Individuals enrolled in Medicaid can obtain transportation (non-emergency medical transportation, or NEMT) to their Medicaid-covered appointments as part of their benefit, while individuals who are not insured, insured through Medicare, or who have private insurance are responsible for their own ride. The Americans with Disabilities Act (ADA) requires transit agencies to provide paratransit for individuals who are not able to use the fixed-route bus (guidelines for eligibility are set at the federal level and made more specific by individual agencies). Paratransit service must be available during the same hours as fixed-route service and available to pick individuals up and drop them off up to three-quarters of a mile off of the fixed route. Veterans have access to transportation to U.S. Department of Veterans Affairs (VA) health care facilities; more than 100 of the 153 VA

[1] The workshop is part of a project sponsored by the Federal Transit Administration.

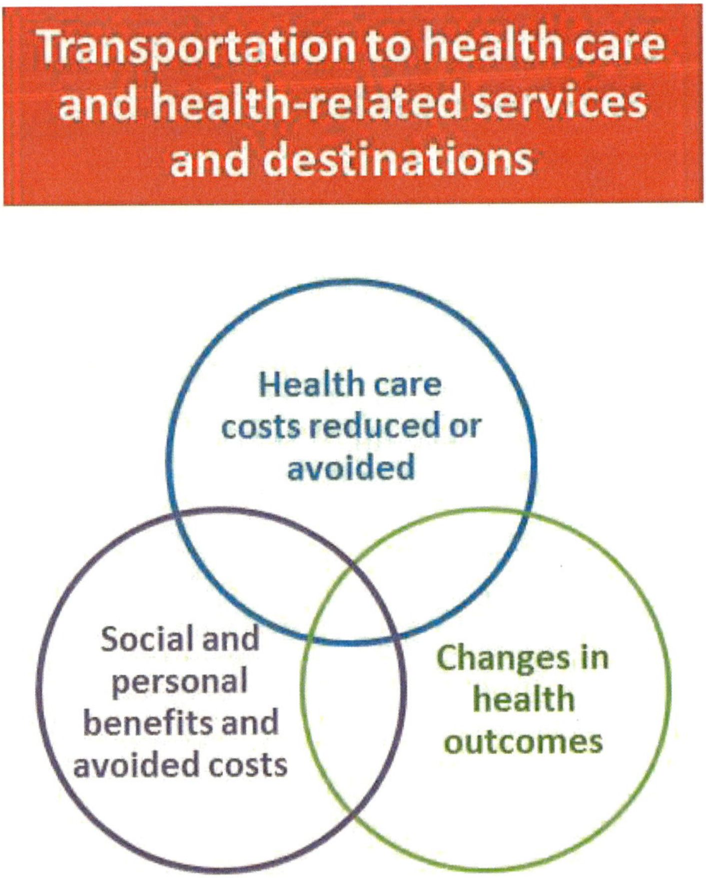


**FIGURE C-1** Selected health-related benefits of transportation access.

health care centers around the country have a mobility manager on staff to help veterans access transportation. Through the Veterans Transportation Service (VTS), veterans can access a ride to the VA from a central meeting point. Enrolled members of a federally recognized tribe have access to health care through Indian Health Services (IHS). The structure of IHS-funded clinics varies, and many provide transportation services to members in need who are not eligible for Medicaid or VTS.

Even with transportation benefits, Medicaid patients and paratransit riders experience many of the same barriers as non-NEMT and non-paratransit patients. Medicaid transportation does not include trips to the pharmacy or grocery store, for example, and some patients may not have transportation options that match with their health care needs and schedule. Individuals needing paratransit service may need to access a destination outside of three-quarters of a mile from the fixed route or may need assistance getting out of their home or getting settled into their health care facility (transit providers can decide if they provided curb-to-curb or door-to-door service but generally do not cross the threshold of the door). If a veteran needs assistance in getting to the VTS meeting point, or, for example undergoes an outpatient surgery that prevents driving back home from the meeting point, then VTS will not meet his or her needs. Enrolled members of a federally recognized tribe may technically be able to access health care at an IHS-funded clinic, but their transportation options could range from assistance from a Community Health Representative (who may be unable to transport them when they need it), to tribal or other transit service, to Medicaid or VTS, to nothing at all. Because NEMT is a Medicaid benefit that is regulated by the Centers for Medicaid & Medicare Services (CMS), the ADA paratransit is regulated by FTA, the Veterans Transportation Program is managed by the VA, and tribal transportation funding is set aside and regulated through the federal transportation bill each service must adhere to different rules and regulations, and each service generates trip data.

While many patients travel to health care outside of NEMT, paratransit, veterans' services, and tribal services, these four services are of particular interest when examining the return on investment of transportation access to health care. These four services are provided to some of the most medically vulnerable individuals, for whom access to transportation to health care can often mean the difference between managing an illness and developing multiple chronic conditions or ending up in the emergency room, between living independently and moving to assisted living, or worse.

Past studies have attached a financial cost to transportation barriers to health care, based primarily on missed appointments and on emergency department use and hospitalizations resulting from lack of primary and preventive care.[2,3] These costs to the health care system and to patient health are predicted to increase as the U.S. population ages and as our chronic disease burden grows. Health care providers increasingly recognize that transportation is a significant barrier for many patients. Accordingly, we would expect an investment in transportation access to health care to result in benefits for the health care system and for patients. Because trans-

---

[2] Wallace, R., Hughes-Cromwick, P., Mull, H. 2006. *Cost-Effectiveness of Access to Non-emergency Medical Transportation: Comparison of Transportation and Health Care Costs and Benefits, Transportation Research Record:(1956)*. Pp. 86-93.

[3] Cronin, J., Hagerich, J., Horton, J., and Hotaling, J. 2008. *Florida Transportation Disadvantaged Programs: Return on Investment Study*. Tallahassee: Florida State University College of Business.

portation and health care each manage a different transportation-related program, though, the financial benefits of one program investing in transportation may accrue to another program.

Transportation and health care providers operate under a different set of rules and regulations and have a different vocabulary to define their work and clients. These different vocabularies affect, too, what it means to examine the return on investment of providing transportation services to health and health-related destinations. How transportation and health care professionals define each concept—what is meant by health outcomes, health care savings, transportation, and return on investment—will have an impact on how data are collected and analyzed. Many interviewees discussed how to define return on investment relative to their specific program aims, citing health care savings, improvements in health outcomes for patients, and other societal and personal benefits that may be realized over a long term and/or otherwise difficult to measure or monetize. Many of the interviewees contacted for this report are engaged in some way with NEMT services. While the original contact list did not include a disproportionate number of NEMT-related contacts, interviewees often suggested additional contacts involved in NEMT. One reason may be the perception that NEMT programs:

- require specific data collection and reporting;
- are required to implement least-cost solutions; and
- have recognized gaps that may affect the cost of health care;
- making NEMT programs a likely starting point for many health care and transportation partnerships.

## Health

The World Health Organization (WHO), in 1946, defined health as a "state of complete physical, mental, and social well-being and not merely the absence of disease or infirmity."[4] This definition is widely accepted and has been in place for 70 years.

Moving from a definition of health focused on an individual to the health of populations, in 1988, the Institute of Medicine described public health as "what we as a society do collectively to assure the conditions in which people can be healthy."[5]

As our understanding of the factors that influence health grows, medical health and public health professionals are recognizing their shared

---

[4] See http://www.who.int/about/definition/en/print.html (accessed September 27, 2016).

[5] See http://www.nap.edu/catalog/1091/the-future-of-public-health (accessed September 27, 2016).

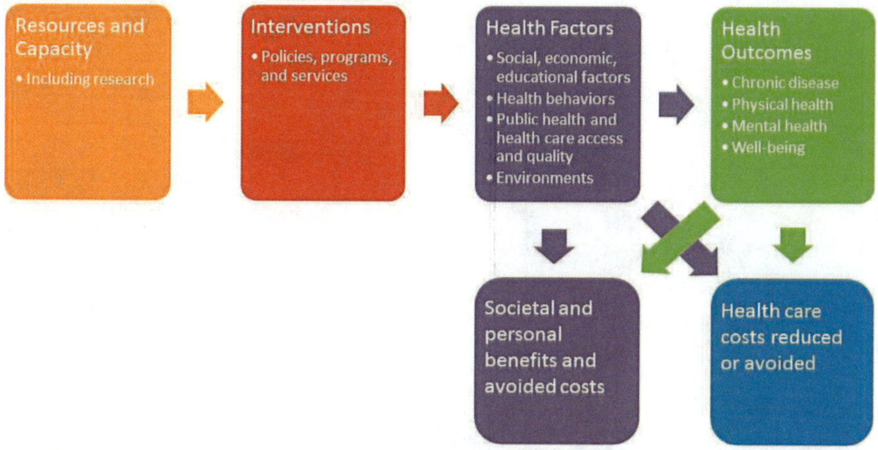


**FIGURE C-2** Transportation access to health care logic model. Based on models from County Healthy Rankings (http://www.countyhealthrankings.org/our-approach) and NASEM, 2016.

roles in improving patient outcomes. Public health logic models attempt to capture the relationship among resources, programs and policies, health factors, and health outcomes (see Figure C-2 for a logic model for transportation access to health care). Resources and understanding help drive interventions, in turn changing health conditions that impact health outcomes. Improvements in health outcomes and improvements in some health conditions may result in reductions in health care costs. In addition, both health conditions and health outcomes may result in societal and personal benefits and avoided costs that may never be directly reflected in health care costs.

For this environmental scan, the interventions we focused on are transportation policies, programs, and services to improve access to health care and health-related goods and services. Outside of the context of this environmental scan, interventions could include anything that may result in improved health factors—from violence prevention and immunization programs to building more sidewalks or increasing affordable housing supply. This wide range of possible interventions reflects the wide range of health factors that determine individual (along with population) well-being.

You may notice in Figure C-3 that another important health factor—genetics and biology—is not included in this model. Because the model (and this scan) focuses on the impacts of policies and programs, genetics and biology is not included. Also notice that clinical care is shown as being

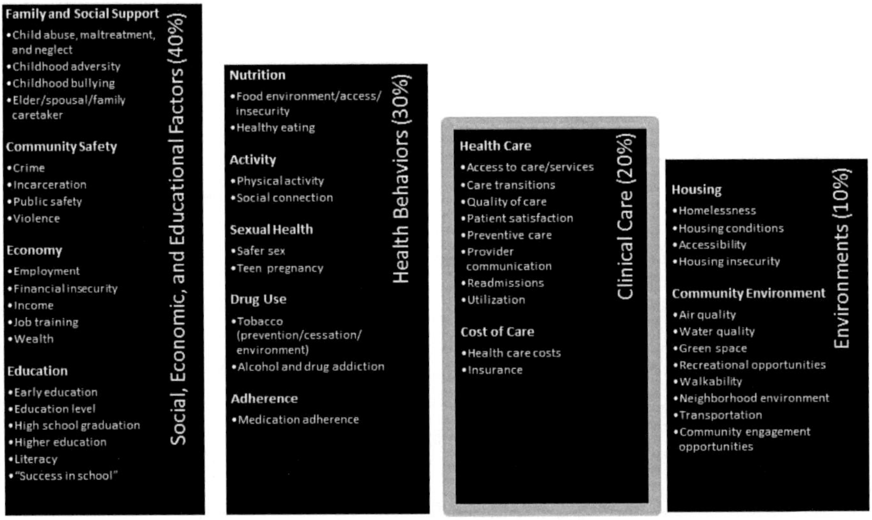


FIGURE C-3 Health care factors and proportion of impact on health outcomes. Revised from County Health Rankings model (http://www.countyhealthrankings.org/our-approach [accessed September 27, 2016]) and 100 Million Healthier Lives Measurement System: Progress to Date (http://www.100mlives.org/wp-content/uploads/2016/04/IHI_100MHL_Metrics_SpringGathering_ONLINE.pdf [accessed September 27, 2016]).

responsible for about 20 percent of the impact that policies and programs have on health outcomes. While this factor includes "cost of care," with respect to individual health outcomes, "cost of care" here means cost to the patient. However, in considering cost savings to health care providers or insurers, factors included under "clinical care" are relevant. Figure C-3 is not comprehensive; instead, it is focused on factors most relevant to transportation and health care partnerships.

This environmental scan did not include transportation programs solely designed for social and recreational purposes, though a growing body of research indicates that these trips are important for maintaining health and some interviewees, especially those working in rural areas, mentioned isolation as an important health factor. Consider again the WHO definition of health provided earlier: "state of complete physical, mental and social well-being and not merely the absence of disease or infirmity." A recent report from Martha McClintock and colleagues for the *Proceedings of the National Academy of Sciences of the United States of America* indicates, "there has been little rigorous scientific attempt to use [the WHO definition]

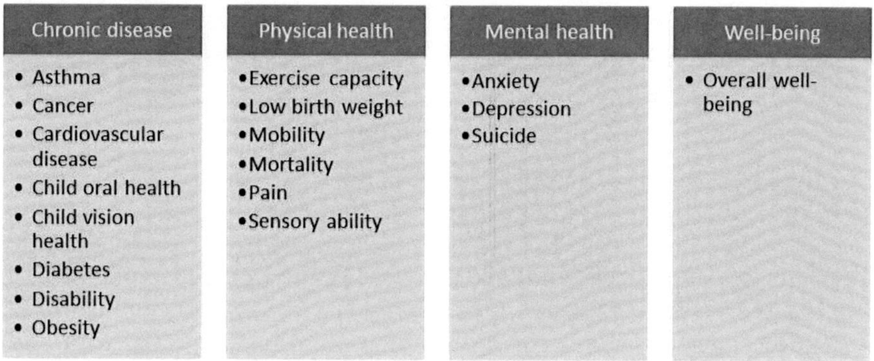


**FIGURE C-4** Health outcomes related to transportation access to health care.

to measure and assess population health. Instead, the dominant model of health is a disease-centered Medical Model, which actively ignores many relevant domains."[6] Using medical, psychological, and health data from the National Social Life, Health, and Aging Project, McClintock and colleagues found that "specific medical diagnoses (cancer and hypertension) and health behaviors (smoking) are far less important than mental health (loneliness), sensory function (hearing), mobility, and bone fractures in defining vulnerable health classes" for older adults. Figure C-4 shows some the main health outcomes impacted by transportation access to health care. This list reflects outcomes discussed by interviewees as well as outcomes suggested by McClintock's work and a national health improvement initiative.[7]

Health care and transportation partnerships explored through this environmental scan do not directly measure the results of transportation investments in terms of improved health outcomes. Instead, measurements are often focused on utilization of primary care, emergency room utilization, hospitalization, transportation trips provided, and other data directly related to the provision of transportation and care. Although health care providers may have data on patient health outcomes, interviewees noted the difficulty of understanding the impact of transportation on access to care and the resulting impact of care on health outcomes. Interviewees expressed

---

[6] See http://www.pnas.org/content/early/2016/05/10/1514968113.full.pdf (accessed September 27, 2016).

[7] Adapted from 100 Million Healthier Lives Measurement System: Progress to Date (http://www.100mlives.org/wp-content/uploads/2016/04/IHI_100MHL_Metrics_Spring Gathering_ONLINE.pdf [accessed September 27, 2016]) and McClintock et al., Empirical redefinition of comprehensive health and well-being in the older adults of the United States (http://www.pnas.org/content/113/22/E3071.full.pdf [accessed September 27, 2016]).

a desire to better understand the connections among transportation access, care access, and health outcomes experienced by clients.

## Transportation

Transportation encompasses a broad range of infrastructure, services, policies, and programs—from walking on city sidewalks with curb cuts that accommodate mobility devices to trains, airplanes, trucks, and barges that carry freight across the land, air, and sea. For the purposes of this scan, we focused on transportation providers, services, or programs that either primarily transport people to health care or for which access to health care or health-related goods and services is an important component. To more easily consider available data sources and possible partnerships with health care, it may be helpful to categorize transportation on a continuum of modes of transportation and the various entities that plan, design, operate, and maintain these various modes. Figure C-5 below presents a collection of entities involved in various elements of the transportation continuum. Each of these is also supported by a network of roads, sidewalks, and paths that are developed and maintained by a combination of entities ranging from state and local governments to private developers.[8]

Transportation programs included in this scan focused most often on Medicaid clients accessing Medicaid-covered health services. Other populations often discussed included dialysis patients, veterans, people experiencing multiple chronic conditions, pregnant women, children, individuals accessing drug treatment programs, older adults, and people living in rural areas. Several interviewees discussed the importance of transportation in alleviating social isolation and noted how difficult it can be for many clients to have access to transportation to get out into their community outside of medical trips.

## Return on Investment

Return on investment (ROI) is a kind of cost–benefit analysis traditionally measuring financial returns (or gains) compared to resources invested. For example, ROI has been used to determine the effectiveness of research and development or marketing efforts for businesses. More recently ROI has been adapted to examine social and environmental impacts through Social Return on Investment. For the purposes of this scan, we began by thinking of investments in terms of (funding for) transportation access to

[8] Revised from FLPPS Transportation Committee Executive Summary, personal communication. (Committee information can be found at: https://flpps.org/Workstreams/Transportation, accessed October 25, 2016.)

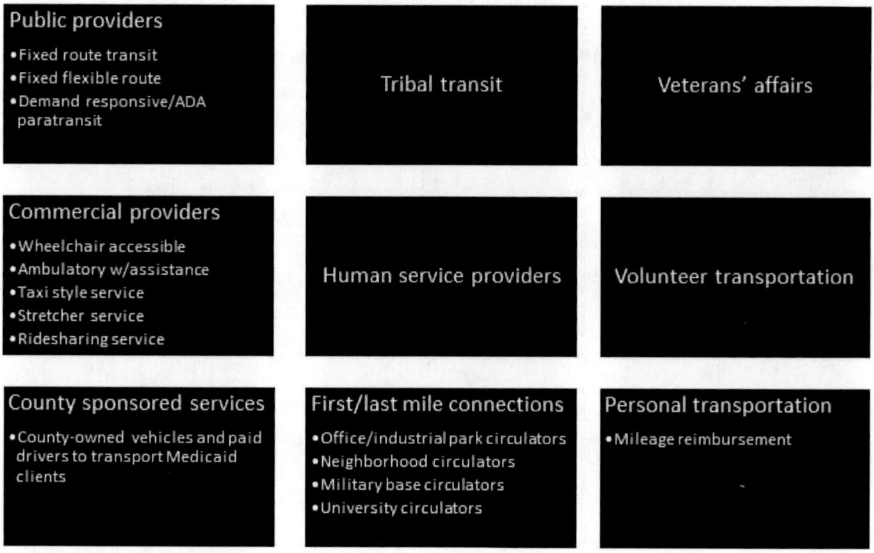


**FIGURE C-5** Transportation services related to access to health care.
NOTE: ADA = Americans with Disabilities Act.

health care and returns in terms of health care savings or avoided health care costs. We were also interested in efforts to track changes in health outcomes related to transportation investments.

One of the first steps in determining ROI in any context is understanding the outputs and how those outputs translate into returns. For example, transportation providers typically report on:

- fare revenue
- passenger trips
- project revenue miles
- deadhead miles[9]
- total project miles
- vehicle service hours
- volunteers
- vehicles
- incidents
- injuries
- fatalities

[9] The miles a vehicle travels when out of revenue service.

These outputs are helpful to transportation in measuring a journey, but alone they are not sufficient to understand the full impact of transportation, or what happens after the journey.

For this scan, we were interested in learning about partnerships to connect these outputs to returns through reductions in health care costs. Unfortunately, several challenges emerged through the interviews:

- such data are not readily available from all transportation providers;
- existing data are insufficient to account for important context, such as the population density of the area served; and
- even if a health care partner can attribute health care savings to a trip provided (for example, by using an estimate for missed appointments), it can be challenging to allocate the right proportion of the relevant transportation metric to that trip.

Similar challenges exist on the health care side of the equation. Interviewees most often mentioned staff capacity and technology as the primary barriers to solving the first two challenges. To address the third challenge, one strategy often used in ROI analysis in other sectors is cost allocation, which would allow transportation providers to better understand the cost of providing each individual trip. While nearly every interviewee recognized some benefit to understanding the monetary benefits to health or health care of investing in transportation access, few programs were able to measure this directly. Even without this information, though, several transportation and health care partnerships are moving forward with a shared understanding that monetary benefits will emerge.

## INTERVIEW BACKGROUND

Nearly 70 individuals were interviewed for this environmental scan. The interviewee selection is not representative of all of the relevant expertise on this topic. Interviewees represent a diversity of organizations and roles within those organizations—from federal agencies to local providers and community-based organizations, from individuals who distribute funding to those who managed programs and work with individual patients or clients. For a list of individuals interviewed, please see p. 160. Throughout the scan, direct quotes from interviewees will be used as examples of the major themes. In order to protect privacy and to encourage honest and candid information sharing, quotes will not be attributed to a specific individual. Instead, quotes will be followed by the sector in which the individual works:

- brokerage
- consulting/technical assistance
- consumer/consumer advocacy
- foundation/funding
- health services
- human services
- research/academia
- transportation services
- tribal transport/health care
- veterans' services

Interviewees were asked about health and transportation partnerships that they knew of or worked within; business models that supported those partnerships; and the data collected, analyzed, and shared through those partnerships. Interviews were conducted primarily by phone and lasted 15–60 minutes. Interviewees were asked to suggest other potential interviewees as well.

Overall, among interviewees there was an appetite for better understanding the data and evaluation measures being used or under consideration in other areas—whether those areas are disciplines, geographic areas, or specific programs. There was an accompanying sense of trepidation about the limitations of examining the costs and benefits of transportation investments in relation to health care.

Interviewees expressed gratitude to FTA for funding this workshop and the other related efforts examining the intersections between transportation and health care, and several suggested areas where FTA and other federal agencies could support local efforts to coordinate and improve service provision.

## SUMMARY OF THEMES

Across sectors and other variables like geography and client demographics, interviewees shared many of the same challenges and potential solutions. Overall, the most significant challenges interviewees face in creating health and transportation partnerships and measuring return on investment fall into seven categories (not listed in order of importance):

1. Defining return on investment
2. Funding and basic infrastructure
3. Missing information and data
4. Technology

5. Geography
6. NEMT destination and service gaps
7. Cross-sector collaboration

Within each of these themes, sub-themes emerged, which are highlighted in each theme's section.

Solutions and opportunities emphasized by interviewees fell into eight categories (also not in order of importance):

1. Grants
2. Shared learning
3. Start small and go slow
4. Let patients tell the story
5. Take the care to the patients
6. Customer experience
7. Sharing resources, increasing revenue
8. Sharing data, analyzing solutions

Fewer sub-themes emerged during discussions about solutions and opportunities.

## INTERVIEW THEMES: CHALLENGES

### Defining Return on Investment

Interviewees, identified below only by their sector, discussed the concept of return on investment from many perspectives, citing challenges and opportunities for how to explore this topic in the future. Major concerns included

#### *Value or Return on Investment Outside of Health Care Costs*

Interviewees agreed across the board that investments in transportation are critically important to supporting access to health care, but they did not all agree that improving transportation access to health care would necessarily result in reduced health care costs.

> "We want to comment on the assumption about reducing the health care cost. Our position has always been that these are areas that are significantly underserved. . . . You're introducing more patients, more frequent patients—could lead to more than just screenings and regular doctor appointment. It could lead to specialty visits." –Transportation services

> "This whole notion that we're going to reduce the transportation costs if we work more collaboratively—I don't agree with that. We're very efficient." –Transportation services

Interviewees suggested that between existing patients accessing more care and new patients beginning to access care, health care costs may increase, at least in the short term (see time scale comments below) and maybe for the long term as well.

> "This is like a sieve—you create a little space and there's lots more need. No matter what we're doing, the more access we provide, the higher the cost will be, because we're not providing for all of those needs now." –Transportation services

> "You're getting people access to surgeries and other care they couldn't get before. So the trade-off is that, for us, we see hospitalizations go up, because we are getting people access to care. But they need that care." –Health services

Some interviewees suggested that measuring benefits in monetary terms obscures the real measure of success—improved access to care and patient well-being—and may not reflect desirable outcomes achieved.

> "If your investment is in health outcomes and not profit, then why are we even talking about this? [Patient's] life improved, quality of life improved. So why are we talking about it as only monetary? Investing in patients is good in and of itself." –Transportation services

> "We're not trying to keep people from health care, so that's not really the cost we want to look at. Are we adjusting medication or treating someone after a stroke? Is it making a difference for you, individual person who received a ride? Transportation providers—are you giving more rides because the system is more efficient? Health care providers—are you noticing fewer no-shows?" –Human services

> "We do show that they got care they wouldn't have otherwise gotten. We worry about the people who never get connected—at homeless shelters, etc. They're not even showing up in the health care system yet at all, and maybe we can keep them out of the ER?" –Health services

### *The Time Scale Over Which We Measure*

Many interviewees suggested that, while health care costs may be reduced as a result of better transportation access to care, these benefits might not accrue in the short term or even the medium term. Interviewees suggested several ways that high care costs could be reduced with increased transportation access to primary care, from preventing emergency room visits to increasing the time a person can stay in his or her own home.

> "Even though we're always concerned about the trip costs, at the same time, we're trying not let lack of transportation become a barrier to successful treatment. Often [patients] will come in in a very vulnerable state. It takes a while before they have success with their behavior changes . . . and we can start getting them to drive again or figure out other transportation. Sometimes that takes time, and it's worth the higher cost investment to get them to that point." –Brokerage

> "It's like everything in life—you have to put in up front to get a return on the back. What we do costs more up front. Up front that first year or two out of the facility costs more than being in, but after that, the costs fall off greatly once a person is established at home. We talk all of the time about how much cheaper it is for an individual with a disability to live in the community than in a facility, but it costs more to actually get them there." –Health services

> "One of the things that we really believe, is that what we do supports people living in place, decreases isolation, so they're less likely to go to an assisted living facility." –Transportation services

### *Return on Investment for Whom*

Interviewees described many benefits of improved transportation access to health care and health-related destinations that will not necessarily be reflected in health care costs. This topic generated some of the richest feedback from interviewees, providing ideas for future study.

#### For the Patient

> "Our program encourages states to look at inclusion post-discharge. Rather than just moving somebody, and then you're on your own. . . . We encourage our grantees to tell us how they're going to encourage people to get involved—something to get them out of the house and be part of the new community" –Health services

> "Indirect route and the long wait times were concerns [for patients], because they have to dialyse for so much of their life already, having to add an hour or two increases the time that they're all about dialyses and not about their life. . . . 'I need to go home, take a nap, so when my kids get home I can make dinner and be part of their lives.' Doesn't have a cost that can be quantified with money." –Transportation services

## For Caregivers and Family

"[There was a] gentleman who needed to go to bariatric treatments three times a week. His wife had a disability, and he took care of her. If he hadn't gotten reliable transportation, his wife would have had to go into assisted living. Who knows what would have happen to his wife if he hadn't been able to get that transportation." –Human services

"[Could we quantify] family costs, such as costs saved because family members who are caregivers can return to work and/or engage in family activities because their role as caregiver diminishes as their loved one gets well?" –Human services

"Caregivers often quite frequently die before the people they're caring for; so the ripples [of giving them a break from transportation] are spreading throughout the community and is ultimately just a win for everybody." –Transportation services

## For the Community

"It would be great to quantify: economic contribution of individuals because they can get to work; increases on workforce participation for those individuals who coordinate transportation service or provide the rides directly; decrease in lost productivity costs for employers—reduction in need to hire temporary employees; increased production or service; decreased health insurance costs; community costs—costs on community integration, participation in religious and civic organizations. People who are healthy can spend money in the community, participate in community recreation and entertainment events, they can vote, they can attend events (that might have entry fees), etc. Could these costs be captured?" –Human services

"[Patients using ambulance for nonemergency transportation] may put other people at risk, too. If they're bringing people to nonemergent medical appointments, that keeps them from being able to provide emergency care." –Research/academia

"If we have patients who are abusing drugs, they're going to have myriad health conditions. Their children are going to have health issues, domestic violence issues, going to be in jail all of the time—it leads to societal issues as well as health issues" –Health services

# Funding and Basic Infrastructure

Interviewees consistently talked about the need for more funding to effectively meet the needs of clients and patients. In response to having too few resources, interviewees emphasized two major themes—going slow and starting small—that will be addressed in the "Solutions and Opportunities" section. In addition to the nearly unanimous call for more funding generally, individuals working with tribal transit and tribal health care highlighted the need for basic infrastructure on tribal lands.

> "When [other provider] is talking about the sheer danger of being on the roads, it's very real. The only road into their community is a 36 mile dirt road. To have a school bus driving on that road is scary. Anyone who needs higher medical care than their clinic can provide [to get there] is scary. Getting food in—18 wheelers on that road—is scary." –Tribal transport/health care

> "Sometimes [water] trucks crash, or there's a flash flood and folks can't get through. EMS services—sometimes the ambulance can't even make it over their roads." –Tribal transport/health care

> "With respect to transportation for Indian country, to be quite honest, it's not just access to the automobile that would get them there, it's about the roads and whether they're passable—whether they can even get there, and if they'd want to risk getting on those roads." –Tribal transport/health care

## Missing Information and Data

Another significant theme across interviewees was related to whether and how relevant questions about access were being asked at all levels of service. Several interviewees working in health care and transportation partnership noted that their work was catalyzed or informed by community needs assessments.[10] Sometimes these needs assessments included questions about transportation, and other times participants brought it up on their own. Others noted that health care providers may not have information about a patient's transportation barriers or if an appointment was missed due to transportation. For tribal transportation, data concerns were primarily focused on crash and other safety data and on GIS data.

### *Asking the Right Questions*

> "Sometimes the patient makes us aware of transportation issue, but other times they won't voice that need if they're not asked." –Health services

[10] Such assessments are an Internal Revenue Service requirement for not-for-profit hospitals and health systems, and are also required of public health agencies by the state or for the purpose of obtaining public health accreditation (see, for example, https://www.nlm.nih.gov/hsrinfo/community_benefit.html and http://www.phaboard.org/accreditation-overview/getting-started [accessed September 27, 2016]).

> "What we found when we asked initially, a lot of them didn't even know why people weren't showing up for their appointments." –Human services

> "We've learned many things such as the anxiety that people have, of using public transportation, for behavioral health" –Transportation services

> "We already had a one-call center. What we didn't have was the mechanism to identify the at-risk patients to address re-hospitalizations." –Health services

> "Regional hospital did the community health assessment but didn't ask about transportation. People would hand write in the margin—access, language barriers." –Transportation services

> "You call to make a doctor's appointment. The very first question is 'What insurance do you have?' We want the second to be 'What kind of transportation do you have?'" –Consumer/consumer advocacy

> "If you use a lot of transportation (not counting dialysis), what are people actually doing when they're using a large amount of transportation? Does that mean anything or not?" –Transportation services

> "Ask outreach programs what they think their needs are. Our sense is that with health center data there's a bias, based on patients that are already walking into the health center doors. For folks not accessing the health care system, the only folks who might have a sense of those barriers are outreach workers. They directly interact or observe some of the groups that don't go to the health centers." –Consulting/technical assistance

Some interviewees noted that it is insufficient to just ask whether or not a patient has transportation; the accessibility of that transportation in terms of culture and timing might have an impact on health care accessibility as well.

> "How well are health centers asking that question? They're not always realizing what options are out there. Need the partners to ask the question in a culturally competent way, in a way that really collects information that we're looking for over time." –Health services

> "The need for same day service is huge—now they can go to the doctor if the doctor will accept them." –Transportation services

> "We are a city of bridges and tunnels and rivers. It's no big deal to cross two bridges and go through a tunnel, but for some people it is [a big deal]. You need to get a handle on the culture of a place as well." –Consumer/consumer advocacy

> "Moms who are at risk of going pre-term, they have to get a progesterone shot to help them get along as far as possible. They can only get it from a compounding pharmacy—only three of them in the region, most in the suburbs. It's a weekly shot. You're only going to pay to get to the doctor; it's important, but the shot is just as important in getting her to full term. If [her] level of comfort to get on the bus (if she can afford it) to go up to this working class pharmacy to get this shot—it's just not going to happen. Gets into race and affordability. . . ." – Transportation services

### *Impacts of the Patient Protection and Affordable Care Act*

One challenge to measuring return on investment that many interviewees noted is the impact of health care transformation. With an increase in the number of people with private insurance and eligible (in many states) for Medicaid, costs are likely to go up in the short term, making it difficult to evaluate a return on investment. New patients may require education about their benefit and other service to help them fully access care, and these costs may impact a provider's ability to evaluate a return on investment as well.

> "[Measuring is] further complicated by the ACA and whether or not the state expanded its Medicaid program. There may be an increase in cost—is that a function of delivery of transportation or simply more individuals eligible. What if medical services aren't available [nearby], and transportation costs increase for that reason?" –Research/academia

> "Ramping up for health care coverage, but for the groups most in need, having coverage was not the same as having access; [there's] distrust and fear in the system (based on immigration, race) and transportation barriers." –Consulting/technical assistance

> "With the ACA and the expansion, we have this population that came on to a plan. A lot have never had insurance and need education about benefits, how to utilize insurance." –Health services

### *Same-Sector Information Gaps*

Interviewees discussed data-sharing challenges not just between transportation and health care but within each sector as well.

> "Information on the transportation side of trips—some of that data is out there, we don't necessarily have access to it. On the medical side, we can see outcomes of people. What's missing is how to connect a person's health to their transportation, so that when transport is identified as a barrier or

need, the health care center can make sure they're providing the right kind of transportation to that care."

"There's a Medicaid broker who helped try to arrange transport. [Patient] had a behavioral appointment that Medicaid would cover. Their doctor said [patient] can take public transit. Their counselor said [patient] needs taxi service because of anxiety. The broker sides with the physician (or the cheaper form of transportation). Sure enough, [patient] doesn't get to their appointment." –Health services

"Trying to figure out how much money it costs for a pre-term birth, that info is not public. Negotiated rates with the insurance companies—[health care providers] won't give that; but also, that's not necessarily the costs. We're only including the hospital stay [in our return on investment evaluation], but you get billed by hospital, doctor, everyone who worked on you. [We] couldn't keep track of everything—we'd have to ask each of the individuals. So we need to have a relationship with the insurance companies to get them to tell us what's being saved." –Foundation/funding

### *HIPAA*

The two biggest challenges interviewees mentioned around data was related to the Health Insurance Portability and Accountability Act (HIPAA). Many interviewees have decided to forgo working through processes related to HIPAA and instead use data related to trips or other non-health proxy data.

"The thing about HIPAA—in small towns, everybody knows who you are if you dig into it enough. [Maybe it should be] us feeding the hospital the transit data and them doing the analysis without talking about the people—just a higher-level aggregate." –Consulting/technical assistance

"If they had told us, 'Here are our top ten ER utilizers, go out and serve them. . .,' but none of our partners would share anything meaningful with us because of HIPAA." –Transportation services

### *Data on Tribal Lands*

Interviewees working in tribal transportation and health care discussed the challenges of funding and operating transportation infrastructure and services without basic data that other sectors often take for granted—crash statistics and GIS in particular.

"When the state divvies up dollars, a lot of times they will exclude tribes, not intentionally, for a couple of reasons: they really don't think about it, and tribes aren't sharing their crash data or don't even have crash data. So even when the tribes do ask for money to improve the roads, the state doesn't see the data to justify why they need the money to improve the roads." –Tribal transport/health care

## Technology

Technology was cited as a barrier to partnership and a tool to improve partnership and data sharing. In particular, interviewees noted the need for data standards and flexible and open software to support for partnerships. Even if an agency is up-to-date technologically, clients may not be able to access the technology due to a lack of awareness or because of their own technological limitations.

### *Need for Standardized Data and Open Technology*

"Modern data standards, well-documented code—allows us to plug and play different solutions as needed. Everything changes so fast, and we need to be ready to meet those needs as they come. Doesn't necessarily mean it has to be open source, but it does have to be developed in a way that is flexible enough to tap into new technology and data sources." –Consulting/technical assistance

"A lot of it goes back to the transit program having the correct technology to dispatch their drivers on time and to the right location." –Tribal transport/health care

"One of the biggest struggles working with the public transit providers and using fixed-route service is a lot of them don't have OS data or GTFS files. [There's] no one-stop shop nationwide so I can appropriately identify the trips and geocode them. Having access to OS GTFS data could make all of the difference in the world in regard to NEMT using the fixed route services. We would be open as a brokerage to exploring the option of helping these agencies create this data." –Brokerage

"You get all of these little proprietary systems. How do you collect data when they don't connect with each other? The FTA or some federal agency [could take] the lead and make open source platforms, standards." –Transportation services

### *Client-Side Technology Barriers*

"[We're doing] one year of planning to make sure our technology will serve the needs of the individuals in the center for independent living—

individuals who are unable to see or hear; will it work with the reader devices, etc." –Brokerage

### *Tracking Trips*

The difficulty of tracking transit trips emerged as a concern primarily related to NEMT but also in general for considering return on investment. The potential of electronic fare to enhance trip tracking was discussed by several interviewees.

> "Public transit agencies (don't know if they're carrying a veteran or a NEMT trip)." –Research/academia

> "One thing we found, especially in the public transit system, it can be difficult to track who is riding and what kinds of needs they have. If you don't have a card that identifies who the riders are, then the systems are not able to identify with great accuracy. They can probably make decent estimates of what riders fall into what categories, but if you're looking at a short period of time at increasing ridership, that can be challenging." –Consulting/technical assistance

## Geography

Challenges related to density of population and different kinds of service boundaries were a common theme among interviewees.

### *Rural Challenges*

Interviewees noted that transportation and health care needs and appropriate measures of success are different for rural areas, compared to urban and suburban areas. Interviewees also noted that much of the transportation need in rural areas is related to health care.

> "Transportation for us is really a problem in rural areas. When people want to transition back to their home on a farm, the state has to give us a 24 hour back-up plan. So states are slow to move people back to rural areas; [they do] not want them to move from a facility back into seclusion." –Health services

> "There are very different issues in the rural and non-rural areas. The metrics around transportation needs some component to take those into account. How are you using resources efficiently if there are only seven people per square mile? That's something we're finding. We have the numbers for each site; when we look at number of rides, distance of trips—the more rural the site, the less efficient the transportation is. Unless that is

pointed out to leadership, they just think that the program isn't functioning well." –Veterans services

"They had to start with criteria that said less than seven people per square mile. What about the rural parts of neighboring counties, say three people per square mile, but the county average brings it up? We've driving right by people who should have access." –Veterans services

### *Jurisdictional and Service Boundaries*

While barriers in each state differ, interviewees across the board experienced challenges crossing service or political borders. Interviewees expressed frustration at not always knowing who was imposing the boundaries and what could be done to better integrate neighboring systems.

"All of the sudden you have this brokerage in [Town A] trying to get someone to [Town B] and back. How do you even out the cost? Basically [you] need to have agreement between each of the transportation providers." –Consulting/technical assistance

"You have to be certified by each of the providers, pay whatever rate each charges. That's a huge barrier as far as independence. You can only go as far as my service goes—beyond that you have to work with another provider." –Health services

"We had to get federal motor carrier authority to be able to take folks to the clinic in [other state]. We were the first transit agency to go through that process. No one really knew how to do it, and [we] had to get transferred so many times, because they don't know their own rules. It took us a year." –Transportation services

"That whole issue of not being able to cross lines or borders without those agreements—I understand that intellectually. But is there something they can do to make that easier? It's ridiculous. I can get my patient to the border, but then I have 2 miles to go, and I have to get someone from another county. Is it a statutory requirement? A funding requirement? If you're going to have regional health care, there's got to be some way to make this a little easier to do." –Health services

"Health care did not have the capacity to take people to regional care. We need to cross 1, 2, or 3 municipal boundaries, and the original model was designed for local rides on a recurring basis." –Human services

## NEMT Destination and Service Gaps

These issues were raised generally and in relation to Medicaid, Medicare, and VA transportation. Interviewees described several health-supportive destinations that they considered to be key factors in improving health outcomes, including pharmacies, group homes, support groups, grocery stores, assessment appointments, and benefit qualification meetings. Some interviewees also discussed difficulties arising from children and caretakers not being able to ride along with patients.

> "The big one that we always hear is pharmacy; there are tricks to get your prescriptions on your way home from the doctor." –Health services

> "Even groceries—some [patients] can get them delivered, but many do not have this option. You're at a severe disadvantage to maintaining yourself at home if you can't even get food." –Research/academia

> "You have to have a face-to-face with a physician to say you need home services—well that requires transportation to get there in the first place!" –Research/academia

> "Transportation is an issue, too, at the point of preparing to transition. We have to get people to Social Security offices, get them to go and view places they can live. If they're not part of the paratransit system or any number of [other barriers]—if they can't easily get to and from where they need to go to make the transition process happen, it makes things more difficult." –Health services

> "We started a rides to grocery program. We had mom and pop stores closing and nowhere to buy groceries. Rides to groceries was designed to provide options and hope for people. Little were we aware of the linkage between fresh fruits and veggies and health care. We have many partners in that program." –Transportation services

> "A lot of nonprofits have rules about not going to group homes, but a lot of group homes don't have vehicles." –Brokerage

> "Even one of our local assisted living programs doesn't have an ADA vehicle. They won't buy one—we've tried to sell them one." –Transportation services

> "A lot of these patients wouldn't have had any appointment for behavioral health [without our program] because Medicaid doesn't cover the initial assessment." –Human services

> "The thing I hear the most is we have free Medicaid transportation, but I can't bring my kid. I can't get a babysitter for them." –Foundation/funding

## Cross-Sector Collaboration

### *Cross-Sector Knowledge*

Interviewees described hurdles to collaboration, including confusion around language, funding sources, how different programs operate, how to connect with the right individuals in other sectors, and what programs might be appropriate to partner with. These same concerns were echoed during the Improving Healthcare Outcomes: The Mobility Management Connection symposium during the 2016 Community Transportation Association of America (CTAA) expo in Portland, Oregon. The following quotes are from interviewees, not CTAA participants.

> "It would be ideal if CMS and FTA could get together and put together a common language or corresponding language." –Brokerage

> "If the state DOTs could have sort of 'go-to people' lists available for the transit agencies that are out there in their respective states. Even within the agencies that should know their own rules, there's a lot of misinformation out there." –Transportation services

### *Different Motivations and Measures of Success*

Several interviewees suggested that diverging missions or measures of success create significant barriers to effective partnerships between health care and transportation.

> "We find that both public transit and Medicaid NEMT have a similar goal—they want to provide individuals, especially those without other options, access to health care. And there's an expectation that it will improve outcomes. Beyond that, they don't have many additional goals or objectives in common, and in fact they sometimes diverge." –Research/academia

> "Health care operators are always going for the least cost, trying to drive down the cost as much as they can—including transportation. Or, there are some saying 'what if we provide all these access and support services so people can be healthier? Will that reduce our costs?' CMS is driving both of these models at the same time." –Consulting/technical assistance

> "The two professions come at this from a very different perspective. The public transit arena would like to think that through coordination and shared trips that they're capable of providing the lowest cost, most effec-

tive transportation. But from Medicaid, the transit agency is not always lowest cost. So you see the evolution being more and more brokered through a private broker and capitated payments, so there's not a link to the trip provided and the payment made. And the private broker is looking to make the trip at the lowest cost, maintaining their contract, and making a profit margin. Public transit agencies with fleet replacement, advanced vehicles, technology, etc.—not necessarily seen as valuable to the Medicaid transport folks. Public transit seeks to recover its operating costs, but the Medicaid brokerage is really just looking for the cheapest; [there is] not consistency about those objectives and how to measure them." –Research/academia

"There's a contradiction in the NEMT language. It encourages demand response trips as a last response. They encourage people to use public transportation to the maximum extent possible, but if that happens, there's no way to track that trip. Maybe you provide a fare ticket or a fare card; short of a smart card, you can't track it. But that's the lowest cost for everybody. NEMT—they encourage it, it's in the language, but there's no effort to require that or to document, to evaluate an individual or their trip and then send them that way. You'd think brokers would encourage that since it lowers their cost, but they can't track the encounters, so that's counter to their mandate to track data." –Research/academia

"The people that are most interested are the payers—the insurance and the managed care folks; not really the health care providers." –Transportation services

"Until transportation becomes an incentive measure, then we wouldn't have a real frequent process of looking at that. We do look at people who are the most fragile who go to the ER a lot or access care a lot. We do reach out to them to see what their needs are—that's one thing [readmission] that is an incentive measure, and transportation is part of that." –Health services

"Transit people have [an] assumption that more access and more rides are better. People paying for health care (mainly Medicaid, since they pay for transportation) embrace attitudes of insurance company—'the less we have to pay, the better, so more transportation is the opposite of better.'" –Transportation services

One issue that interviewees mentioned repeatedly was that a strong emphasis on fraud prevention on the health care side might be hindering more effective partnerships between health care and transportation providers. The challenge seems to be ensuring proper use of funds and services while maximizing benefits to patients.

"Medicaid funds have to be used for a beneficiary who needs to get to an approved medical trip and no other purpose. They can't be on a bus with a veteran or someone else. It creates a perverse incentive for some successful programs to not chat with researchers about what is actually working and successful if it fits into a grey area. If you're trying to do something innovative that just works for your patients, not trying to break federal grant rules, you may want to avoid having to ask forgiveness. They may not even know they're in violation." –Research/academia

"In the VA, folks are very concrete. They're worried that the veterans are just saying they needed [the transportation program] because they like the service." –Veterans services

"Public transit is looking to provide any users transportation for any trip purpose in the most cost-effective manner possible. NEMT is looking to get Medicaid eligible people to Medicaid eligible appoints for the cheapest cost. [Medicaid is] really looking to prevent fraud and abuse—including using transportation for any other trip purpose, even shopping. Doing so, even as trip-chaining, would be considered fraud or abuse." –Research/academia

### *Coordination*

Interviewees noted that coordination improves as it is mandated, and several commented on the importance of coordination at the federal level.

"Coordination mandates need to be happening on both sides. Right now, that mandate is on the DOT side from the FAST Act, but it needs to be mandated for other folks spending money on transportation and flow down to the states and regional coordination. Medicaid sends the money to the states, and the states have great latitude to spend this money. They have no ultimate obligation back to adhere to coordination or the intent to work with local public transit agencies to work effectively with resources." –Research/academia

"When brokerages were just getting established [health services] came out very strongly that brokerages were creating a siloed system—they already had a state coordinating council. [Recently] they said that brokers are helping facilitate, but it's due to some of the state requirements for coordination." –Research/academia

"Over 80 programs provide funding for transportation disadvantaged populations, around 40 or so federal programs that provide [NEMT] funding. [Where is] data on the programs, on the number of people they provide services to, which grantees, how much funding is being used." –Research/academia

"This is going to sound way out there. It just seems to me we have so many rural veterans in this country, it would be nice if CMS could partner with the VA to leverage some of those transportation resources. They drive right by and even go through the same community." –Research/academia

"My experience with Medicaid is that it's one of the areas where it was hard for people to understand. [The Medicaid NEMT provider] can transport people to VA medical centers, and it's a covered service from the perspective of transportation. From the visit side, there's not encounter data—it's not available. That does create some issues if you're audited. But you're helping a veteran get to the care that's more appropriate and allowable. It creates a little discomfort." –Health services

"[We're] like 5-year-olds playing soccer—everyone storms around the soccer ball and are all trying to do the same thing, not aware of what other people are doing and when to pass the ball." –Health services

### *Change Takes Time*

"We're learning we have to really start small. The willingness, for people to change and organizations to change—it's really hard to do. The idea that we'd make suggestions and wave carrots and people would change isn't really happening." –Health services

"When you're bringing worlds and disciplines and sectors together, it's not the easiest natural place for people to go. Give adequate time and space to understand each other's language, build trust; it takes time, intentionality, real management whether at the highest level or within community. Be mindful of the longevity of the effort, what it takes in terms of the active management could be easy to overlook if you're just looking at it as part of the data and programmatic end." –Foundation/funding

"It always takes more time to develop the connections than you can ever plan for. If you don't take time to do that, you're basically putting together a program. A program can never address a complicated social issue. Five years later, everybody's going to look back and say, well that didn't really work. You have to develop a lot of trust to be able to work together; it's not for the faint of heart. We've certainly seen some people drop off who have no tolerance for that type of work. We would have just continued to meet and admire the problem from year to year and not changing it." –Human services

"We've been working with [software company] for about 3 years to purchase our product for our call center, making significant customizations. After we began working with [Coordinated Care Organization], they required us to have a business associate agreement with any of our contractors, especially if sharing data. It took us 18 months, but we finally got a signed business associate agreement with [software company]." –Brokerage

"I got all of the groups to come and meet and talk. 'We're in competition with each other for funding—your passengers aren't going to ride in my vehicles.' It's changed so much since then, but it's taken a lot, and some people are still not willing to look at new ideas." –Brokerage

## INTERVIEW THEMES: SOLUTIONS AND OPPORTUNITIES

### Grants

Several interviewees viewed the Rides to Wellness and other grant opportunities as catalytic in the creation or progression of partnerships between transportation and health care.

"This opportunity came, a real reason to work with the transportation folks. We didn't have them on our coalition. [Rides to Wellness] is what created that impetus." –Foundation/funding

"These [projects] emerged from the conversations we had even prior to applying for the grant. After applying for the grant, were able to form partnership more coherently." –Brokerage

### Shared Learning

Interviewees relayed a need for more and better systems for sharing learning relevant to this topic. Several mentioned having met peers at conferences or learned about other projects through grantee meetings. Many interviewees suggested areas where it would be beneficial specifically to have more guidance from the federal agencies, including related to funding streams and associated rules and the Stark Law.

"[There is a] need for more knowledge management in this area—we have a tendency to have great ideas, implement them, someone comes in and tries to make it more 'efficient' and then basically blows it up." –Consulting/technical assistance

"It's now easy for us to look at these things, but prior to doing this work we wouldn't have thought about it. And that's how we can contribute—help folks to start seeing—'Oh, my peer did that.' Otherwise we get really dismissive. If people see organizations like theirs tackling these challenges—that's the importance of the peer-to-peer learning groups." –Consulting/technical assistance

"Brokerage [is] operating under 'you have to be 18 to get your own approval to get transportation for health care, to get approved for health care.' The law says as young as 12 you can receive health care without guardian permission." –Health services

"[Health services] really hold their hat on this [Stark] law that prevents them from paying for transportation. We believe that's just an interpretation." –Transportation services

"They can ask for things in their states plan in the way they execute their Medicaid program, likely to be approved in an individual level. Just because someone doesn't think the funds can be used that way, sometimes they can. How it plays out on the local level is completely locally driven." –Research/academia

## Start Small and Go Slow

By far the most commonly discussed theme across all interviewees was the amount of time that transportation and health partnerships and programs take to build. Interviewees suggested several different reasons for and benefits of going slow. Because the need for transportation to support health is so great, some programs suffer from trying to grow to quickly or setting out to solve too many issues at once. Several interviewees noted how difficult it can be for individuals and communities if a transportation program disappears or is scaled back.

"The goal is 1 year of planning to make sure our technology will serve the needs." –Brokerage

"It was meant to be a small thing, and it grew too much. It turned into something bigger than we expected." –Transportation services

"[We're] definitely trying to control the growth, because we're still learning and there's a lot we don't know. The bigger we get too soon, the capacity becomes an issue." –Human services

"We are focused on a part of our state that by all indicators really needs help. It has been the beneficiary of a lot of programs saying 'We're coming in with the answer to your problems.' [There was] not a lot of buy-in from the local folks. [Our] core element at this point is planning—not ready to run out and develop a service, say 'Here is the answer.' Lots of outreach is needed in this initial buy-in to avoid push back and avoid low utilization." –Transportation services

"Without success, we won't get the other folks to the table to support us. That's why we are narrowly focused." –Transportation services

"We had to keep scaling down this program, because the demand was so much greater than the money we had." –Transportation services

"Those [Rides to Wellness] projects that focused on information and outreach actually seemed like they had a good first step to the future work they might be doing. Those that were trying to come up with new models of service coordination or service provision—some are going to work out, but it's more aggressive and had more risks along the way. To try to change how to provide what we're providing, this stuff takes time. A lot of times people are surprised by that." –Transportation services

"For last 2 years, [we've been] laying foundation for starting the partnership with the transit agencies and reaching out to bring awareness to the benefits of partnering with the NEMT brokerages—for us, them, the members they serve." –Brokerage

"We have always had an historic partnership with the [program]. It's been the paratransit service's largest customer for the last 25 years. I was in a meeting when we were faced with this issue. The design challenge email came through the next day, so we started working on it." –Transportation services

"One thing that's come out of this to me that's been worth all of the time we put into it—we have built the greatest partnerships in this community to understand health care and how we can all work together." –Transportation services

"We have access to our leaders; you can just pick up the phone. Maybe if you had asked me about that 5–6 years ago prior to [project], I might not have said that. Since we've gone through such a strong exercise of building the [project], it keeps the partnership going." –Transportation services

"Make sure you know everything else that is going on in your community. You may be duplicating efforts, you may be so overwhelmed with demand that your great idea becomes more of a headache than anything else, and you're still turning people away left and right. Know who you're going to serve, who you could not service through the program. If you want to develop an effective program serving the population you want to serve—reach out to them and ask them what they need, what they'd like to see, what are the problems they've encountered, how can you ensure whatever gets built, provided, funded in the community addresses those needs." –Consulting/technical assistance

Most interviewees expressed a need for more resources, but many also discussed the need to work with available resources—from funding to community assets—in the short term, while future financial funding is unknown or unstable. This theme is closely related to the next theme, because many interviewees viewed working with current assets as the most sustainable way to begin new partnerships or programs.

> "What we see so often is that things develop quickly without a sustainability plan. How can we be sustainable as funding comes and goes, while we make something that's reliable and a utility for people? Our users rely on us—we can't just go away next year. Innovation is the hot thing, but what can we do to support, grow, and amplify the things that already exist." –Consulting/technical assistance

> "If someone would just give us a lot more money we could do this or that. But that's not coming soon, so what are we prepared with right now with what we can provide? How can we do that most collaboratively with what we have right now? How can we best get the results we need with what we've got?" –Transportation services

> "Some partnerships formed, a lot [are] in the beginning stages. We talk about fixed-route services first. That was the first piece, work with transit agencies all across the county, identify members who can use fixed route services and are within .75 miles of a stop." –Brokerage

### Let Patients Tell the Story

Several interviewees emphasized the importance of listening to patients' stories and working with patients to help develop programs and resources. Some interviewees had been able to previously develop video or Photovoice[11] projects and found them to be very valuable for both the patients to share their perspective and for the organizations to make progress in funding or otherwise supporting partnerships and programs.

> "We talk internally about how important it is to talk about this from the perspective of the patients. The solutions are about people." –Consulting/technical assistance

> "If you're talking to 20 providers, you should talk to 20 consumers." –Consumer/consumer advocacy

[11] A definition of the Photovoice process is available at http://ctb.ku.edu/en/table-of-contents/assessment/assessing-community-needs-and-resources/photovoice/main (accessed on September 27, 2016).

"What needs to drive what we collect and track and use to make decisions is the relevance to the individual—to their needs and if those needs are being met. The person being served is at the center of how we're collecting this data and how we're using this data. Quantitative data isn't enough—we need to know how their quality of life is being impacted." –Transportation services

"We [dialysis patients] make a huge impact [talking to decision makers]. It's not just a story for them—I'm real. It's not 'There's 270,000 of us [dialysis patients].' I try to put a face to it—we're real." –Consumer/consumer advocacy

## Take the Care to the Patients

A few interviewees mentioned existing or planned mobile units to respond to transportation barriers. These existing and planned units have foci ranging from children's health and adult primary care to behavioral health crises and hospital discharge follow-up. One interviewee recommended creating a mobile pharmacy.

"The plan once we get it up and running is to have a list of people who have been discharged from our hospital during the week, and [mobile unit] would go out within 2–3 days to visit them and make sure things are going well. They're able to intervene within a limited scope to prevent readmission, funded through the cascade health alliance." –Health services

"In the aftermath of CHIP passage, the period of time after the money had been given out, [there was a] lag in uptake in certain states. We put two mobile units in the deep South, heard from a lot of concerned folks—that while they were excited about the prospects of having kids enrolled, a lot of them were experiencing long-standing transportation barriers and rendered their newly gained insurance coverage not as useful as it should have been." –Foundation/funding

## Customer Experience

Customer service was a common theme among interviewees, with several noting the value of the extra training that public transit staff complete. In all regions, but especially in more rural areas, interviewees noted the benefit to clients of having regular drivers, volunteer or paid, with whom the patient develops a relationship.

"Working with insurance companies, drivers have HIPAA training—extends from the health insurance companies but is a different model. Client base is vulnerable in some way, so the drivers need to be altruistically motivated, customer service based." –Brokerage

"One plan originally didn't offer public transit, and now it's the highest utilized option. Members have been happy, complaints have gone down, and they're saving money." –Brokerage

"The small public transit in rural areas are people-focused and community-focused. From a brokerage perspective, it's good to have people on the ground providing services for you." –Transportation services

"The other element [to address] from a federal perspective—our customer is the same customer as a public transit customer. From Medicaid and FTA—anything we can do to make it easier to access those services is good. A lot of times we're all serving the same customer, the payment and eligibly is different; are there ways to make that easier for the customer?" –Transportation services

"We'll send as many trips as possible over to [public transit], and we get reduced complaints, better member service." –Brokerage

### Sharing Resources, Increasing Revenue

Although most interviewees described challenges in creating partnerships that involved cost sharing, several also shared examples of early partnerships that included in-kind donations of staff time and other resources. Cost allocation was suggested as one tool to help transportation and health care partnerships better understand inputs and outcomes to measure return on investment. Some transportation services staff discussed the revenue benefits of working more closely with health partners in terms of Medicaid transportation trips, too.

"One of the things I did at the brokerage was to try to support the public transit agencies to contract with us, keep them busy. The Medicaid transportation became an additional source of revenue that supplied match for the federal grants. I viewed that as being a win-win any time I could partner with those types of organizations." –Transportation services

"We run the fixed-route bus service; also run the NEMT brokerage for the three counties—whatever is needed to get them to their health care appointments. That's become a real big business for us dollar wise—bigger than general fund." –Transportation services

"Program of all inclusive care for the elderly—we are the only type of transportation provider to provide this transportation service in the country. [The] operation is part of the local hospital. They pay the full cost of the rides. Through the contract, we provide the vehicle, the driver, and an attendant on board, through your door to help and through your door to the health service. To the degree that the hospital is benefiting in their model and they utilize us, we can capture our full cost of providing that trip. It allows us to expand service without expanding the local subsidy." –Transportation services

"Individual people who are eligible for these services—they know if they have an expectation for a demand response trip they can get it. Why bother with rail or bus in that case? In some environments, they know that the public transit agency is the option of choice, and they choose to just use fare—that means that the transit agencies doesn't get the extra money they would from Medicaid (even though it saves Medicaid money from the demand response)." –Research/academia

"[We] launched a call center with a marketing team of board members and marketing director from [health services]—their phones, their computers, their office supplies—that's their match. Expenses are my salary and the operating costs. [Health services] is doing all of my accounting and HR; I am a [health services] employee leased to [brokerage]." –Brokerage

"Our DOT public transit division is very supportive of the work we do. I've heard others talk about their 5310 money and how difficult it is to access it and use it—it's often focused only on capital purchases. [The DOT public transit division has] receptiveness to maximize the use of federal dollars by leveraging state money and trying not to leave anything on the table. Regionally, having a transit agency willing to step outside of the box—using private, state, and federal programs—and having a transit authority that understands that public transit goes beyond a fixed-route system and beyond ADA is a benefit in our community." –Transportation services

"The transit system has allowed the health workers to go on the bus with patients without charging us to get people used to it. Don't know what that cost is to the transit agency." –Health services

"First year of the [community health worker and transportation] program was funded by [CCO] as part of transformation money, now expired. Then the hospital took over the program—staff [is] hired by them and works for them." –Health services

"[We have] two significant partnerships—both regional hospitals. As they looked at access, they saw loss of efficiency in the process by not having a centralized on-site presence to coordinate that effort. They both contract with [brokerage] and pay for a staff person to coordinate transportation; large part is Medicaid transportation, but it does spill over to non-Medicaid clients also. So we have staff there on site to coordinate the transportation. They were able to demonstrate that in having that presence they were able to free up medical staff time to get out of the business of transportation. Rather than the social workers, discharge nurses doing it—now it's transport staff." –Brokerage

"Most of the operators had a positive experience—did it at a fully allocated cost. Role of NEMT has been leavening for rural transit has allowed rural communities to do amazing things." –Consulting/technical assistance

"From the transit's perspective, by setting up this model, compared to what it would have been if we had done it the traditional way of more individual rides which we are obligated to do, we're saving between $25,000 and $30,000 a month." –Transportation services

## Sharing Data, Analyzing Solutions

While interviewees discussed many hurdles to sharing information between health care and transportation providers, some solutions emerged as well, ranging from Business Associates agreements to meet HIPAA requirements to housing transportation staff within the hospital or clinic. Others offered options for avoiding HIPAA issues by asking patients directly for information; some of these same solutions are included in the next section—"Available Information."

"Main programming is the navigator, and the navigator will work for the clinic. [Nonprofit organization] will bring the coalition together, hire someone to analyze the data we get, but the clinic is going to implement the program. [This structure] got us a lot of things—they can watch someone from the day they walk in to the day they deliver, can follow people and see what their birth outcomes are, how are people who use the navigator working out, compare that to outcomes for people who aren't using the navigator." –Human services

"We also got a grant from [funders] who have come together looking at technology to get data. We're going to collect feedback from patients through SMS. After somebody goes through the program, they'll get a text, and we'll ask them questions and get feedback outside of HIPAA. We'll get information from them pretty close to the time they're receiving the services; [a nonprofit organization] will be collecting that data—more about customer service than outcomes." –Human services

"Some benefit to the transportation benefit being part of the CCOs—which is ultimately having the information in the same place will help be able to address those questions better." –Transportation services

"[Health care providers] were very concerned about customer confidentiality and HIPAA. We clearly defined to them what the pilot would include—data sharing on customers that opted in. They'd be completely notified. We did incentivize it, because we asked participants if they were opting in to complete a pre-, post-, and quarterly survey. [Health care provider] was provided documentation on what the pilot would look like. There was a champion—a social worker who acted as the bridge and agreed to help facilitate the gathering of patient information. They agreed to let us have everybody's prescribed treatment times and monthly or quarterly documentation on the actual time on the machine so we can compare those." –Transportation services

"Going to track over time evaluation measures—mental and physical health (self-report). Since they're going to get transit passes, we're going to track where they use them and how often they use them." –Transportation services

Some interviewees noted that brokers are or could be collecting and analyzing data in a more sophisticated way then other service providers. These data may be difficult to access, though.

"[Brokers] have more data than anyone we've ever seen. Even your small broker serving a small county has more information on individual riders—trends, cost, location. Brokers are the ones that are profit driven, so they're really forced to collect that information." –Research/academia

"[We] could potentially ask the clients themselves with notifications at the end of the trip. Or a phone call for individuals who do not use a smartphone to book their trip. Not just ask them about their trip but how they feel about their health; don't want to collect specific information about the location of the doctor." –Brokerage

"There is data sharing between us and the client [the health plan]. We do monthly dashboards; we're pretty tight with the data we share outside of our clients. [We] don't post average trip costs or how many trips we're serving, but we have provided data for specific research projects that may come up." –Brokerage

## AVAILABLE INFORMATION

Interviewees shared information about national datasets or other relevant information that are currently available and will be available in the future. This section also includes representative snapshots from on-the-ground providers about information being collected at the local level.

## Existing National Data

*Integrated National Transit Database Analysis System*
*http://www.ftis.org/INTDAS/NTDLogin.aspx*

> "[RTAP] surveys the state DOT programs nationally and the transit program managers in states every 2 years. We ask them about their service and their issues. It gives us a clear picture of the challenges and issues that are relevant to our audience. We also ask about how they train and their technology. Rural operators and states have to report significant data as part of their grant agreement with FTA. National RTAP funds an analysis site so that systems and states can compare themselves and their numbers with other entities in the state and nationally." –RTAP

*General Transit Feed Specification, Google*
*http://maps.google.com/landing/transit/cities/index.html#NorthAmerica*

> "Lists the cities that have fixed-route service and accesses their itinerary builders. This gives you a picture of the availability of fixed-route transit in any given area of the use. Some states have taken more of a leadership role in assisting rural operators in becoming visible through Google maps." –RTAP

*National Transit Database*
*http://www.ntdprogram.gov/ntdprogram/data.htm*

> "Metrics: trip data, costs, revenue hours, revenue miles, vehicle miles, passengers per hour. These data elements can be down loaded from the NTD webpage or sliced and diced through the link I gave you. We are working with one of our board members who is going through an analysis process to identify health cost savings with enhancing access for people who are managing chronic illnesses." –RTAP

*AGing Integrated Database*
*http://www.agid.acl.gov/DataGlance/SPR*

AGID is an "online query system that provides access to ACL-related program performance results, surveys and other data files." Users can examine data, by state, that includes Census databases and Administration on Aging (AoA) databases. AoA databases include State Program Reports (SPR), Title VI Services by Tribal Organization, and Long-Term Care Ombudsmen reports. The SPR data may be of particular interest to health care and transportation partnerships. It includes information about one-way trips funded through the Older Americans Act, including demographic information about clients, client satisfaction, federal dollars spent, and the services accessed, including

- Personal Care
- Homemaker
- Chore
- Home-Delivered Meals
- Adult Day Care
- Case Management
- Congregate Meals
- Nutrition Counseling
- Assisted Transportation
- Health Promotion
- Cash and Counseling

–Administration for Community Living

*NORC (National Opinion Research Center) University of Chicago*
*National Social Life, Health, and Aging Project*
*http://www.norc.org/Research/Projects/Pages/national-social-life-health-and-aging-project.aspx*

> "The health of older adults is influenced by many factors. One of the least understood is the role that social support and personal relationships play in health and aging. The National Social Life, Health, and Aging Project (NSHAP) is a longitudinal, population-based study of health and social factors, aiming to understand the well-being of older, community-dwelling Americans by examining the interactions among physical health and illness, medication use, cognitive function, emotional health, sensory function, health behaviors, social connectedness, sexuality, and relationship quality. NSHAP provides policy makers, health providers, and individuals with useful information and insights into these factors, particularly on social and intimate relationships. The study contributes to finding new ways to improve health as people age.
>
> To date there are two waves of NSHAP data available to researchers, and funding has now been awarded for a third wave of data collection. In 2005 and 2006, NORC and Principal Investigators at the University of Chicago conducted the first wave of NSHAP, completing more than 3,000 interviews with a nationally representative sample of adults born between 1920 and 1947 (aged 57 to 85 at the time of Wave 1 interview). In 2010 and 2011, nearly 3,400 interviews were completed for Wave 2 with these Wave 1 Respondents, Wave 1 Non-Interviewed Respondents, and their spouses or cohabiting romantic partners. The second wave of NSHAP

is essential to understanding how social and biological characteristics change. By eliciting a variety of information from respondents over time, NSHAP provides data that will allow researchers in a number of fields to examine how specific factors may or may not affect each other across the life course.

In 2015 and 2016, NSHAP plans to conduct more than 4,800 interviews for Wave 3. In the third wave of data collection, we will interview respondents that participated in a previous wave(s), which will improve the robustness of the study's longitudinal data by adding a third time point. In addition, we will recruit and interview a new cohort of adults born between 1948 and 1965 and their spouses or cohabiting romantic partners to allow us to examine changes in trajectories of health across birth cohorts. As in Waves 1 and 2, Wave 3 will describe health and health transitions of respondents, and how they relate to a different kinds of social relationships in respondents' lives.

For all waves, data collection includes/will include three measurements: in-home interviews, biomeasures, and leave-behind respondent-administered questionnaires. The face-to-face interviews and biomeasure collection take place in respondents' homes." –NORC

*National Core Indicators*
*http://www.nationalcoreindicators.org*

"National Core Indicators (NCI) is a collaborative effort between the National Association of State Directors of Developmental Disabilities Services (NASDDDS) and the Human Services Research Institute (HSRI). The purpose of the program, which began in 1997, is to support NASDDDS member agencies to gather a standard set of performance and outcome measures that can be used to track their own performance over time, to compare results across states, and to establish national benchmarks." –National Association of States United for Aging and Disabilities (NASUAD)

*Data Set Directory of Social Determinants of Health at the Local Level*
*http://www.cdc.gov/dhdsp/docs/data_set_directory.pdf*

–Centers for Disease Control and Prevention

*Health Indicators Warehouse*
*http://www.healthindicators.gov*

Includes Nation Health Interview Survey data among others. –National Centers for Health Statistics

## Coming Soon

### *National Core Indicators-Aging and Disabilities*
### *http://nci-ad.org*

"The National Core Indicators-Aging and Disabilities (NCI-AD) is an initiative designed to support states' interest in assessing the performance of their programs and delivery systems in order to improve services for older adults and individuals with physical disabilities. NCI-AD is a collaborative effort between the National Association of States United for Aging and Disabilities (NASUAD) and the Human Services Research Institute (HSRI). NCI-AD's primary aim is to collect and maintain valid and reliable data that give states a broad view of how publicly funded services impact the quality of life and outcomes of service recipients.

NCI-AD brings an important value proposition to the field of aging and disability services through development of indicators and outcomes that assess quality of life, community integration, and person-centered services. The project will help to address long-recognized gaps in assessing outcomes in long-term services and supports (LTSS) service systems that go beyond measures of health and safety to address important social, community, and person-centered goals as well as quality of life.

Data for the project are gathered through annual in-person surveys administered by state agencies to a sample of at least 400 older adults and individuals with physical disabilities accessing publicly funded services in skilled nursing facilities, Medicaid waivers, Medicaid state plan programs, and/or state-funded programs, as well as older adults served by Older Americans Act programs. The survey instrument includes a background survey, which gathers data about the consumer from agency records, and an in-person survey, which includes subjective satisfaction-related questions that can only be answered by the consumer, and objective questions that can be answered by the consumer or, if needed, their proxy. Project team interprets each state's data and produces reports that can support state efforts to strengthen LTSS policy, inform quality improvement activities, and compare their performance with national norms." –NASUAD

Survey questions include

- Do you have transportation when you want to do things outside of your home, like visit a friend, go for entertainment, or do something for fun?
- Do you have transportation to get to medical appointments/pick up medications when you need it?
- Can you see or talk to your family as often as you want to?

- With "transportation" offered as an option to choose in the follow-up question Why not?

### Existing Local or Program-Specific Data

Most interviewees accessed and analyzed data from one sector. To understand value or return on investment, they rely on aggregate data, anecdotes, or only consider impacts within their own sector. Interviewees use surveys, aggregated data, anecdotes, and already completed analysis from other regions or sectors to help evaluate services and inform decisions.

> "We can say—to what destination are they heading and circle different geographic coordinates. This many trips to hospital, this many to the shelter, this many to the bar—we can code the type of trips and know location-wise where are you going, how many miles, how long to get situated, what kind of money used—state, fed, donations. We do an MOU with all of the folks who have use of our corporate platform." –Brokerage

> "Short-term, [we're] looking at access—number of trips and appointments successfully made. The impact on health care outcomes is going to have to be designed with more guidance from the health care side." –Transportation services

> "We own the software that the brokerage is using; we have access to all of the data. One of the things we want to look at is—how much transportation occurs within an individual's county, and how much takes them outside of their county. [There is] limited information about the appointments in the software." –Transportation services

> "[They] have had increased behavioral health appointments—greater than they've ever had before. People are keeping their appointments; people are getting better and getting better faster. The big thing for the hospital [after a patient is discharged], they have no transportation to go home. The hospital can't get that patient out of the bed, and keeps them from making money. Ability to get patients into a more appropriate setting after their care at the hospital is finished. For each $1 invested you save $9—calculating out the avoided health care cost. That hospital in 2015 had the best financial year they'd ever had; CEO attributed a big piece of that to this project." –Consulting/technical assistance

> "We have a health transportation coordinator paid through [health services], housed in hospital, coordinates rides for a large region, tracking financial impact for each patient. We know what billable revenue has been tied to the patients brought to the door through this project and what it costs us to get them there. The consideration on the health care side—just

because it was billed doesn't mean it was what they netted. We need an actuarial study to figure it out." –Human services

"Number of trips, average fare, what are patients paying—we will collect those data." –Human services

"Did one survey via e-mail veterans. We can take that data and show that, according to the veterans, 25 percent wouldn't have made it to their appointment. What is the cost of a missed appointment? Over a period of time, reducing the number of missed appointments saves the system a lot of money. Missed appointments are a big deal; access to care is limited to the time the clinic has to see veterans. If someone misses and that time goes unused, that's a big deal." –Veterans services

"One study demonstrated that VTS does impact missed appointments. [We did] one round of the survey, and now we're authorized to do a second round. We'll have some numbers that suggest [that] at least." –Veterans services

"I've been told that through the Medicaid brokerage, appointments for preventive care—the no-show rate has dropped. [Have seen] a higher number of patients for preventative, which has overall savings." –Brokerage

"When do people call, what kind of trips are they? Where are they going? What's the ride for? If they're a veteran, if they use a mobility device, their level of service? Not HIPAA related—trying to stay away from that issue." –Brokerage

"When we first started our high-risk pregnancy program, a lot of our moms thought it was normal to take the ambulance to the ER every time they had pain. We've only had 134 people in our high-risk pregnancy program, but only 5 have had low-birth-weight babies. [We've] been able to see that and that there was a cost reduction of about $2,000 per case. Ambulance rides decreased dramatically." –Health services

"The 98 highest utilizers were costing us $9 million, reduced by half. We saved them $2.4 million in ER costs. But this same group at that point only had had 1,500 primary care visits. Once we got them on the bus or [paratransit], their primary care visits increased to 6,500. So higher transportation and some care costs, and lower ED and ambulance usage." –Health services

"The utilization of VA medical appointments has increased; the VA has reported no cancelations for people using this service." –Veterans services

"It's been highly successful with multiple ROI: decrease in no-show appointments, members are feeling more supported and satisfied with health care, 65 members have actually graduated from the program and have met their goals, decrease in emergency room and hospital readmissions, improved appointment compliance, medical compliance." –Health services

"We were a participant for 4 years in a community-based transition program. Our job was to prevent readmission into hospital. Had coaches that met with patients in the hospital and followed them closely for 40 days. Part of that, we gave them the coaching, and we actually gave them free transportation to their follow-up medical appointments, meals, in-home assistance like housekeeping and things like that. We reduced readmissions. [We don't know] if the people who got the transportation access had less missed appointments, more compliance—we didn't really have a good control group." –Transportation services

"In the last 4 years since 2011, the health care authority in [state] has been requiring the brokers to submit a report—data tracking and utilization system. It's an extensive data base getting a lot of trip information for the Medicaid clients using transportation." –Brokerage

"We commissioned a poll and came up with a survey. [We] determined that a significant percentage—20 percent of children under 200 percent poverty and 9 percent under poverty line—were missing routine health care because of transportation barriers." –Foundation/funding

"We do collect data out of that program, but it's principally the number of rides, associated health care visits for primary care and allied support services." –Foundation/funding

## Coming Soon

### *Ride Connection*

Ride Connection, a nonprofit transportation services provider in Portland, Oregon, developed and is implementing a pilot program to improve outcomes for dialysis patients. In June 2016, Ride Connection will have a third round of survey data available. In addition, an article by Ride Connection staff discussing the program will be published in *The Journal of Nephrology Social Work*, National Kidney Foundation: https://www.kidney.org/professionals/CNSW/JNSWOnline (accessed September 27, 2016)

*The Way to Wellville*

> "How do you get to Wellville? There are many roads and help from visionaries who've made great strides creating places where people enjoy healthier lives. Yet the Way to Wellville remains mostly unexplored.
>
> That's why HICCup is sponsoring The Way to Wellville, a national challenge among five communities over five years to make significant, visible and lasting improvement in five measures of health and economic vitality. In the end, we'll map new paths for entire communities to make changes that result in healthier people and places.
>
> Communities were required to submit a completed application in May 2014 to be considered for The Way to Wellville challenge. After reviewing 42 applications from 26 states, HICCup selected the Wellville Five communities in August 2014.
>
> HICCup is a nonprofit founded by angel investor Esther Dyson to encourage a rethinking of how we produce health. Working together in Wellville, we will show the world how collective investment and action can return healthy dividends for communities—and their investors." http://www.hiccup.co (accessed September 27, 2016)

## RESEARCH AND RESOURCES

### Completed Reports

*GAO 12-647 Transportation-Disadvantaged Populations: Federal Coordination Efforts Could Be Further Strengthened*
*http://www.gao.gov/products/GAO-12-647*

Findings: "Eighty federal programs are authorized to fund transportation services for the transportation disadvantaged, but transportation is not the primary mission of most of the programs GAO identified. Of these, the Department of Transportation administers 7 programs that support public transportation. The remaining 73 programs are administered by 7 other federal agencies and provide a variety of human services, such as job training, education, or medical care, which incorporate transportation as an eligible expense in support of program goals. Total federal spending on transportation services for the transportation disadvantaged remains unknown because, in many cases, federal departments do not separately track spending for these services. However, total funding for the 28 programs that do track or estimate transportation spending, including obligations and expenditures, was at least $11.8 billion in fiscal year 2010.

The interagency Coordinating Council on Access and Mobility, which the Secretary of Transportation chairs, has led government-wide transportation coordination efforts since 2003. The Coordinating Council has undertaken a number of activities through its 'United We Ride' initiative aimed at improving coordination at the federal level and providing assistance for state and local coordination. For example, its 2005 Report to the President on Human Service Transportation Coordination outlined collective and individual department actions and recommendations to decrease duplication, enhance efficiencies, and simplify access for consumers. Key challenges to federal interagency coordination efforts include a lack of activity at the leadership level of the Coordinating Council in recent years—the Coordinating Council leadership has not met since 2008—and the absence of key guidance documents for furthering agency coordination efforts. For example, the Coordinating Council lacks a strategic plan that contains agency roles and responsibilities, measurable outcomes, or required follow-up. GAO has previously reported that defining and articulating a common outcome and reinforcing agency accountability through agency plans and reports are important elements for agencies to enhance and sustain collaborative efforts.

State and local officials GAO interviewed use a variety of planning and service coordination efforts to serve the transportation disadvantaged. Efforts include state coordinating councils, regional and local planning, one-call centers, mobility managers, and vehicle sharing. For example, state coordinating councils provide a forum for federal, state, and local agencies to discuss and resolve problems related to the provision of transportation services to the transportation disadvantaged. In other examples, one-call centers can provide clients with transportation program information and referrals for appropriate service providers and mobility managers may serve many functions—as policy coordinators, operations service brokers, and customer travel navigators. However, state and local governments face several challenges in coordinating these services—including insufficient federal leadership, changes to state legislation and policies that may hamper coordination efforts, and limited financial resources in the face of growing disadvantaged populations."

*GAO 15-110 Transportation-Disadvantaged Populations: Nonemergency Medical Transportation Not Well Coordinated, and Additional Federal Leadership Needed*
*http://www.gao.gov/products/GAO-15-110*

Findings: "Forty-two programs across six federal departments—Agriculture, Education, Health and Human Services (HHS), Housing and Urban Development, Transportation (DOT), and Veterans Affairs (VA)—

can provide funding for nonemergency medical transportation (NEMT) service, although NEMT is not their primary mission. Twenty-one of these programs, including Medicaid, are administered or overseen by HHS. The type of funding provided by these programs varies, but includes capital investments (such as bus purchases) and reimbursements of transportation costs (e.g., bus passes). Total federal spending on NEMT is unknown because federal departments do not separately track spending for these services. In some cases data were not available or NEMT was incidental to a program's mission. However, one of the six departments (HHS) was able to provide estimates indicating that its spending totaled at least $1.3 billion in fiscal year 2012—most of this attributable to Medicaid.

Coordination of NEMT programs at the federal level is limited, and there is fragmentation, overlap, and potential for duplication across NEMT programs. The federal Interagency Transportation Coordinating Council on Access and Mobility (Coordinating Council)—chaired by the Secretary of DOT and tasked with promoting interagency cooperation and establishing mechanisms to minimize duplication and overlap of programs for the transportation disadvantaged—has taken some actions to improve coordination, such as developing a strategic plan. The strategic plan identified the council's goal, priorities, and objectives for 2011 to 2013. However, the council has provided limited leadership and has not issued key guidance documents that could promote coordination. For example, the council has not met since 2008 and has not finalized a cost-sharing policy that would allow agencies to identify and allocate costs among programs. GAO has previously found that agencies providing similar transportation services to similar client groups may lead to duplication and overlap when coordination does not occur. This review found instances of fragmentation, overlap, and the potential for duplication, although the extent could not be quantified.

State and local officials in the selected states GAO visited identified a variety of ways they facilitate coordination of NEMT. These include state coordinating bodies (two states GAO visited), regional coordinating bodies (two states GAO visited), local metropolitan planning organizations, and local transit agencies. Cost and ride sharing and one-call/one-click information centers were also used to coordinate NEMT services. However, GAO found two programs—Medicaid and VA NEMT programs—largely do not participate in coordination activities. Requirements to serve only eligible individuals and ensuring proper controls are in place to prevent improper payments and fraud are among the challenges to coordination for these programs. These important NEMT programs provide services to potentially over 90 million individuals and coordination without the Medicaid and VA programs increases the risk for potential overlap and duplication of services."

*GAO 16-221 Medicaid: Efforts to Exclude Nonemergency Transportation Not Widespread, But Raise Issues for Expanded Coverage http://www.gao.gov/products/GAO-16-221*

Findings: "States' efforts to exclude nonemergency medical transportation (NEMT) benefits from enrollees who are newly eligible for Medicaid under the Patient Protection and Affordable Care Act (PPACA) are not widespread. Of the 30 states that expanded Medicaid as of September 30, 2015, 25 reported that they did not undertake efforts to exclude the NEMT benefit for newly eligible enrollees, 3 states reported pursuing such efforts, and 2 states—New Jersey and Ohio—did not respond to GAO's inquiry. However, the Centers for Medicare & Medicaid Services (CMS), within the U.S. Department of Health and Human Services (HHS), indicated that neither New Jersey nor Ohio undertook efforts to exclude the NEMT benefit.

Two of the three states pursuing efforts to exclude the NEMT benefit—Indiana and Iowa—have received waivers from CMS to exclude the benefit, and are in different stages of evaluating the effect these waivers have on enrollees' access to care.

- Indiana's draft evaluation design describes plans to survey enrollee and provider experiences to assess any effect from excluding the NEMT benefit.
- Iowa's evaluation largely found comparable access between enrollees with and without the NEMT benefit; however, it also found that newly eligible enrollees beneath the federal poverty level tended to need more transportation assistance or have more unmet needs than those with higher incomes.

Officials from the groups that GAO interviewed identified potential implications of excluding the NEMT benefit, such as a decrease in enrollee access to services and an increase in the costs of coverage. For example, nearly all of the groups indicated that excluding the NEMT benefit would impede access to services, particularly for those living in rural areas, as well as those with chronic health conditions."

*GAO 16-238 Nonemergency Medical Transportation: Updated Medicaid Guidance Could Help States http://www.gao.gov/products/GAO-16-238*

Findings: "The nonemergency medical transportation (NEMT) benefits offered by Medicare and Medicaid differ. Medicare provides NEMT via ambulance only when other means of transportation, such as a taxi or wheelchair van, would jeopardize the health of the beneficiary. Medicaid

NEMT is generally available for beneficiaries who have no other means of transportation to medical services. States are responsible for the daily operations of their Medicaid programs and have discretion in how they deliver NEMT. Officials from 15 selected states reported using a variety of models to administer NEMT, including transportation brokers, which are entities that contract with states to administer NEMT services.

The Centers for Medicare & Medicaid Services (CMS), within the U.S. Department of Health and Human Services (HHS), oversees Medicare and Medicaid at the federal level, but this oversight varies by program. CMS generally uses regular program integrity activities—such as claims reviews—to oversee Medicare NEMT. Under Medicaid, CMS also uses regular oversight activities, and these include overseeing states' program integrity activities and periodically issuing guidance. However, some of CMS's guidance is outdated or may be of limited use because of legislative and other changes that affect Medicaid and states' NEMT programs. For example, a 1998 guidebook on NEMT contains outdated information on implementing NEMT transportation broker programs. Other more recent guidance is targeted for patients and providers rather than state Medicaid programs. However, these programs also benefit from updated guidance on strategies to ensure compliance with federal requirements while incorporating current practices to meet beneficiaries' needs. Guidance for state Medicaid programs is particularly important because NEMT is at high risk for fraud and abuse; some selected states and stakeholders GAO interviewed reported that updated guidance could be helpful. *Standards for Internal Control in the Federal Government* states that management should ensure adequate means of communicating with stakeholders. Effective communications can take many forms, including guidance. CMS officials reported that the agency is considering assessing whether additional NEMT guidance is needed, but has not set time frames for conducting this assessment.

GAO identified four types of challenges related to Medicaid NEMT and several steps taken by states to address some of these challenges. Challenges reported related to containing costs, maintaining program integrity, contracting with and overseeing vendors, and accessing NEMT. For example, states reported challenges containing NEMT costs due to increased NEMT utilization and reported implementing practices to help address these challenges. Such practices include setting fixed provider reimbursement fees that remained relatively constant in recent years. Officials from 7 of the 15 selected states and 6 stakeholders GAO interviewed reported that having information on how states administer NEMT and ways to address challenges could be helpful to states. Some of this information is available; for example, CMS reported collecting information on states' approaches through state Medicaid plans and posting this information on CMS's website. Other organizations, such as the Transit Cooperative Research Program, have or are in the process of collecting such information."

*TCRP Synthesis 119 Use of Taxis in Public Transportation for People with Disabilities and Older Adults*
*http://onlinepubs.trb.org/Onlinepubs/tcrp/tcrp_syn_119.pdf*

"The objective of the synthesis is to report on current practices, trends, advantages, and challenges of public transit agencies' use of taxis to provide service for people with disabilities and older adults. Public transit agencies are increasingly interested in the use of taxis to serve their riders with disabilities and older adults. Factors contributing to the interest in taxis include the high cost of more traditional small bus and van service particularly for ADA paratransit service, economic strain on public budgets, and the advancement of technology to monitor and verify subsidized taxi trips. As communities and their public transit agencies explore the use of taxis for public transportation, there are lessons to be learned from those who sponsor and subsidize taxi programs for people with disabilities and older adults."

*TCRP Report 173 Improving Transit Integration Among Multiple Providers: Volume 1*
*http://onlinepubs.trb.org/onlinepubs/tcrp/tcrp_rpt_173v1.pdf*

"The purpose of this Manual is to provide guidance to transit agencies; planning organizations; local, regional and state governments; and the array of organizations that are impacted by transit service or have a stake in the provision of transit service, based on the research presented in TCRP Report 173, Volume II.

The research shows that transit integration among multiple transit providers is not necessarily easy, but it is successfully practiced in regions around North America and around the world and yields significant benefits in the communities where it occurs. These anticipated benefits have led some regions to work toward integration of services to create a more seamless system in terms of how riders pay for fares, transfer between routes, and access information about what is available. Indeed, most transit riders do not think of travel in terms of jurisdictional boundaries or agency ownership, but in terms of origins and destinations. Successful integration can create a network that feels unified to the rider."

*National Academy of Sciences Empirical Redefinition of Comprehensive Health and Well-Being in the Older Adults of the United States*
*http://www.pnas.org/content/early/2016/05/10/1514968113.full.pdf*

"The World Health Organization (WHO) defines health as a 'state of complete physical, mental, and social well-being and not merely the absence of disease or infirmity.' Despite general acceptance of this comprehensive definition, there has been little rigorous scientific attempt to use it to measure and assess population health. Instead, the dominant model of health is a disease-centered Medical Model (MM), which actively ignores many relevant domains. In contrast to the MM, we approach this issue through a Comprehensive Model (CM) of health consistent with the WHO definition, giving statistically equal consideration to multiple health domains, including medical, physical, psychological, functional, and sensory measures. We apply a data-driven latent class analysis (LCA) to model 54 specific health variables from the National Social Life, Health, and Aging Project (NSHAP), a nationally representative sample of U.S. community-dwelling older adults. We first apply the LCA to the MM, identifying five health classes differentiated primarily by having diabetes and hypertension. The CM identifies a broader range of six health classes, including two 'emergent' classes completely obscured by the MM. We find that specific medical diagnoses (cancer and hypertension) and health behaviors (smoking) are far less important than mental health (loneliness), sensory function (hearing), mobility, and bone fractures in defining vulnerable health classes. Although the MM places two-thirds of the U.S. population into "robust health' classes, the CM reveals that one-half belong to less healthy classes, independently associated with higher mortality. This reconceptualization has important implications for medical care delivery, preventive health practices, and resource allocation."

*AARP Weaving It Together: A Tapestry of Transportation Funding for Older Adults*
*http://www.aarp.org/content/dam/aarp/research/public_policy_institute/liv_com/2013/weaving-it-together-report-transportation-funding-for-older-adults-AARP-ppi-liv-com.pdf*

"This paper highlights the major sources of federal funding that providers can tap to fund transportation for these populations. As there is no comprehensive dataset that tracks state and local expenditures on specialized transportation, the authors have included seven case studies of local providers from around the country to illustrate how they combine federal, state, and local funding to put quality service on the street. The paper also provides examples of how local and state coordination efforts can expand the reach of services funded."

*AARP Policy Options to Improve Specialized Transportation*
*http://assets.aarp.org/rgcenter/ppi/liv-com/i39-specialized-transportation.pdf*

"The congressional authorization of the surface transportation law, coupled with the growing demand for specialized transportation, presents an opportunity to improve the services targeted to Americans with mobility limitations caused by age, disability, or income constraints. Improvements would allow more of these vulnerable citizens to live in the settings of their choice, including their own homes and communities, and to access employment opportunities in the suburbs that are not well served by public transportation. Given this historic opportunity, the AARP Public Policy Institute is publishing this paper to

- describe specialized transportation, and how it is funded and delivered;
- highlight emerging best practices; and
- offer policy options for improving specialized transportation."

*AARP Expanding Specialized Transportation: New Opportunities Under the Affordable Care Act*
*http://www.aarp.org/content/dam/aarp/ppi/2015/AARP-New-ACA-Transportation-Opportunities.pdf*

"Many states are taking advantage of new options within the Affordable Care Act (ACA) to improve access to care for the chronically ill and to promote community living for older adults and adults with physical disabilities. However, relatively few states are expanding transportation services through these new initiatives for low-income people with mobility limitations. This paper explores the ACA options that could expand specialized transportation for Medicaid and Medicare beneficiaries, and for people who are dually eligible for both forms of coverage. It also provides state examples and two case studies to illustrate how these options can work."

*CTAA Transit Planning 4 All: Inclusive Transportation Planning Grantee Case Studies*
*http://web1.ctaa.org/webmodules/webarticles/anmviewer.asp?a=3265*

"The mission of this project, sponsored by the U.S. Department of Health and Human Services' Administration for Community Living is to demonstrate the value that inclusive processes can bring to transportation efforts.

The Community Transportation Association of America, in partnership with Easterseals, National Association of Area Agencies on Aging, and Westat, is developing, testing and demonstrating ways to empower people with disabilities and older adults to be actively involved in designing and implementing coordinated transportation systems. Our goal is to support communities nationwide in adopting sustainable, scalable, and replicable models that include participation of people with disabilities and older adults in the design and implementation of responsive, coordinated transportation systems."

*FTA Rides to Wellness*
*http://nationalcenterformobilitymanagement.org/rides-to-wellness-home*

"The goals of the 'Rides to Wellness' initiative are to:

- increase access to care,
- improve health outcomes, and
- reduce health care costs.

Through this initiative the transportation community will become a recognized partner with the health/wellness and medical community. This initiative will demonstrate how partnerships across the transportation and health industries can reduce health care costs by leveraging public transportation assets."

*Smart Growth America Metrics for Transportation Investments That Support Economic Competitiveness, Social Equity, Environmental Stewardship, Public Health, and Livability*
*http://www.smartgrowthamerica.org/documents/mndot-working-paper-1-august-2014.pdf*

"This working paper provides a new framework for evaluating transportation projects in Minnesota based on established and emerging practices in the field of public sector teturn on investment (ROI). The working paper is organized around the following chapters:

Chapter 2: Project Purpose and Scope. This chapter describes the context and purpose for Transportation ROI including its relationship to previous and ongoing Minnesota Department of Transportation (MnDOT) work. Ultimately this study may provide direction for implementing a broad based ROI process that helps inform MnDOT's policy and budget decisionmaking.

Chapter 3: Transportation ROI Categories and Metrics. This chapter provides an overview of well-established and emerging approaches to measuring ROI for transportation projects and programs that go beyond safety and system performance. The general categories addressed include

- Economic Competitiveness
- Social Equity
- Environmental Stewardship
- Public Health
- Livability

Chapter 4: Project/Program Selection and Analysis. This chapter considers various options for selecting an appropriate and manageable subset of MnDOT projects and programs that can best serve as a template to test the utility of ROI analysis going forward. It includes a preliminary description of candidate projects/programs followed by a discussion of various options for narrowing the analysis.

Chapter 5: Next Steps. This chapter solicits input from the Project Stakeholder Group (PSG) related to the overall purpose, content, and application of the ROI framework for MnDOT. It also provides a summary of the next steps in this study effort in terms of future meetings and related research and deliverables."

*Economic and Planning Systems Draft Memo on Analysis of Return-On-Investment (ROI) Practices in the United States*
*http://www.epsys.com/wp-content/uploads/2014/08/ROImm0117214.pdf*

"This memorandum is designed to support legislative and other policy initiatives in the State of Washington that advance the effective use of return on investment (ROI) analysis for prioritizing transportation investments. It has been prepared by Economic & Planning Systems (EPS) to support Smart Growth America's ongoing efforts to help states implement innovative transportation initiatives that maximize the benefits of transportation expenditures and grow economies. The analysis is based on a review of national practices and case studies of innovative strategies being employed and various levels of government."

## Reports Under Way or Planned for the Future

*TCRP B-44 Examining the Effects of Separate Nonemergency Medical Transportation Brokerages on Transportation Coordination*
*http://apps.trb.org/cmsfeed/TRBNetProjectDisplay.asp?ProjectID=3541*

"The research is nearing completion. The final draft report is expected spring 2016."

"The objectives of this research are to present options for providing Medicaid-funded NEMT services and evaluate the effects of different options for providing NEMT on: (1) access to Medicaid services; (2) human services transportation (in particular, coordinated transportation services); and (3) public transit services, including ADA complementary paratransit services. The key audiences for this research include state-level policy makers and program administrators and other stakeholders affected by the different options for providing NEMT services."

*TCRP B-45 Transportation to Dialysis Centers: Health/Transportation Policy Intersection*
*http://apps.trb.org/cmsfeed/TRBNetProjectDisplay.asp?ProjectID=4116*

RFP closed 07-13-2016.

"The objectives of this research are to quantify the current and projected demand and associated costs of transportation for kidney dialysis in the United States and identify current effective practices and new strategies for funding and providing transportation for dialysis. The research should address a number of important areas and answer the critical questions presented below. This research should consider and address differences that affect transportation for kidney dialysis in urban and rural areas."

*Health Outreach Partners Rides to Wellness Community Scan*
*https://outreach-partners.org/about-hop/transportation-initiative*

"Will quantify financial impacts of missed appointments.

- **National Survey:** Implementation of a national survey of health centers, Veterans Affairs Medical Centers, and private providers to identify the impact of lack of transportation on health care costs. Key partners include the FTA, the Veterans Health Administration, and UnitedHealthcare.
- **Community Profiles:** Development of profiles illustrating local communities that are adopting transportation solutions that show promising opportunities for return on investment."

*Center for Medicare & Medicaid Innovation Accountable Health Communities Model*
*https://www.grantsolutions.gov/gs/preaward/previewPublicAnnouncement.do?id=55237*

Applications for the Accountable Health Communities (AHC) grant closed in late May 2016. In early 2017, grantees will be announced. The "AHC model addresses a gap in the current delivery system by funding interventions that connect community-dwelling beneficiaries with community services. The AHC model will test three community-focused interventions of varying intensity and their ability to impact total health care costs and inpatient and outpatient health care utilization. This model will engage community-dwelling Medicare and Medicaid beneficiaries of all ages (children and adults)." One of the five focus areas is "transportation needs beyond medical transportation."

*Center for Medicare & Medicaid Innovation Health Care Innovation Awards*
*https://innovation.cms.gov/initiatives/Health-Care-Innovation-Awards/Project-Profiles.html*
*https://innovation.cms.gov/initiatives/Health-Care-Innovation-Awards/Round-2.html*

> "The Health Care Innovation Awards are funding up to $1 billion in awards to organizations that are implementing the most compelling new ideas to deliver better health, improved care and, lower costs to people enrolled in Medicare, Medicaid, and Children's Health Insurance Program (CHIP), particularly those with the highest health care needs.
>
> The Health Care Innovation Awards Round Two are funding up to $1 billion in awards and evaluation to applicants across the country that test new payment and service delivery models that will deliver better care and lower costs for Medicare, Medicaid, and/or CHIP enrollees."

Reports are available for Round 1 projects, and Round 2 evaluation reports should be available soon.

## Tools and Resources

*Children's Fund Health Transportation Shortage Index*
*http://www.childrenshealthfund.org/publications/health-transportation-shortage-index-new-tool-identify-underserved-communities*

> "The HTSI is based on data from a national survey and a regional survey done in the rural Mississippi Delta. The national data show that each year 9 percent of children in families with income less than $50,000 (4 percent of children overall) missed at least one health care appointment annually because transportation was not available. In the regional survey, 10 percent missed a health care appointment because of lack of transportation. In both surveys, nearly one-third of these children later used a hospital emergency department for the condition associated with the missed appointment.

The national survey included a question asking parents if they had difficulty establishing a usual source of pediatric care. A positive response to this was used to identify families with problems accessing child health care services, because difficulty establishing a usual source of care is associated with higher rates of hospital emergency department use for routine illnesses. In the national survey, difficulty establishing a usual source of care was significantly associated with: (1) rural area, (2) low income, (3) longer travel distance to source of care (especially noted in rural areas), and (4) lack of public transportation. In the regional survey, it was associated with not having a car.

Children's Health Fund developed the HTSI to serve as a tool to guide users in the assessment of the most important factors associated with transportation barriers to child health care access. The HTSI factors are: (1) population as a proxy for rural area and for travel distance; (2) poverty as a proxy for automobile ownership; (3) public transportation availability; and (4) health care provider workforce availability. Points are assigned for each factor based on area characteristics and are added together. Higher scores indicate greater risk for transportation barriers to child health care access.

To overcome these barriers, targeted communities should be prioritized for additional public transit resources and/or improved coordination between health care and transportation providers. Some potential strategies are suggested at the end of this report."

*Community Commons*
*http://www.communitycommons.org*

"Community Commons is a place where data, tools, and stories come together to inspire change and improve communities. We provide public access to thousands of meaningful data layers that allow mapping and reporting capabilities so you can thoroughly explore community health.

As a mission-driven organization, the technology and resources that we develop directly provide innovation for the future. We aim to make our custom tools publicly available whenever possible and our partners understand and support this public-good mission."

*National Aging and Disability Transportation Center*
*http://www.nadtc.org*

"To ensure that community transportation services are available to everyone, particular attention should be paid to the needs and preferences of older adults and people with disabilities.

A community's 'family of mobility/transportation options' may include walking, biking, driving, and transitioning from driving, as well as fixed-route public transit, dial-a-ride services, volunteer transportation programs, taxis, and other shared-ride options. In addition, mobility management, one-call/one-click transportation resource centers, and travel training offer person-centered information and assistance that facilitate access to community transportation options.

To accommodate the unique issues older adults and people with disabilities face in accessing and using transportation options, NADTC promotes:

- Engaging older adults and people with disabilities before new transportation options are created and using their insights and experiences to improve transportation programs, design new program,s and ensure that services are of the highest quality.
- Ensuring that older adults and people with disabilities know about the transportation choices available in their community and understand how to access these options.
- Offering one-on-one assistance to assist older adults and people with disabilities to select the best transportation options to meet their needs and use the transportation options available in the community.
- Providing safe, efficient, predictable, and reliable transportation services that older adults and people with disabilities are comfortable using.
- Following the ADA to ensure that people with disabilities are able to stay connected to their communities."

## INTERVIEWEES

| Name | Agency |
|---|---|
| Suzanne Alewine | Missouri Rural Health Association |
| Dr. Chisara Asomugha | Center for Medicare & Medicaid Innovation |
| Erin Barbaro | Institute for People, Place, and Possibility |
| Chris Barnett | Community Commons |
| Diane Barr | Cascade Health Alliance |
| Ed Benning | Mass Transportation Authority, Flint, MI |
| Dr. Julie Bershadsky | Human Services Research Institute |
| Doris Boeckman | Community Asset Builders |
| Carrie Brown | National Indian Justice Center |
| Amy Carmola | United Way of Chittenden County |
| Charles Carr | Mississippi DOT |
| Kathryn Chandler | Northwest Valley Connect, AZ |
| Linda Cherrington | Texas A&M Transit Mobility Program |
| Mary Comtois | United Way of Buffalo and Erie County, Buffalo, NY |
| Dave Cooley | OR Department of Veterans Affairs |
| Troyce Crucchiola | patient advocate, OR |
| Dr. Moumita Dasgupta | Amherst College |
| Kelly Dixon | Greater Buffalo Niagara Regional Transportation Council |
| Virginia Dize | National Aging and Disability Transport Center |
| Esther Dyson | Way to Wellville |
| Jenna Estock | Primary Health Network |
| David Faldmo | Siouxland Community Health Center |
| Kathy Gale | Interfaith Senior Programs, Inc., Waukesha, WI |
| Cheryl Goldstone | Primary Health Network |
| Oscar Gomez | Health Outreach Partners |
| Roy Grant | Children's Health Fund (formerly) |
| Yahaira Graxirena | Central Mass Regional Planning Commission |
| Tabatha Harris | Oklahoma State University, Southern Plains TTAP Center |

| | |
|---|---|
| Jeff Hazen | Sunset Empire Transportation |
| Robert Hicks | Pyramid Lake Paiute Tribe, Transportation Planning Department |
| Joshua Jinks | Finger Lakes Performing Provider System, Rochester, NY |
| Dennis Johnson | Children's Health Fund |
| Angie Jones | Grant County Transit, Oregon |
| Judith Kell | Lakeshore Mercy Health, MI |
| Nancy Knopf | Care Oregon |
| Dr. Alana Knudson | Walsh Center for Rural Health Analysis at NORC |
| Dr. Katherine Kortum | Transportation Research Board |
| Francois Larrivee | Hopelink Brokerage, WA |
| Valerie Lefler | Liberty System, Data & Collaboration |
| Doris Lookabill | OmniRide, VA |
| Kris Lyon | Lane Transit District, OR |
| Heather MacLeod | U.S. General Accounting Office |
| Janet Malley | Whatcom Transportation Authority |
| Randee Mason | PYA Consulting |
| Kelly Myers | National Indian Justice Center |
| Melanie Needle | Chittenden County Regional Planning Commission |
| Alex Page | Ride Connection |
| Ross Peterson | GridWorks, Portland, OR |
| Robin Phillips | National Rural Transit Assistance Program |
| Dennis Presley | Southern Illinois University Center for Rural Health and Social Service |
| Amy Rauworth | Lakeshore Foundation, Birmingham, AL |
| Dr. Marie Raven | University of California San Francisco Medical Center |
| Julia Resnick | American Hospital Association |
| David Riley | Veterans Health Administration |
| Todd Robinson | WSOS Community Action Commission, Inc., Fremont, OH |
| Mark Tadder | CitiCare |
| Frank Thomas | Northeast Oregon Public Transit, OR |

| | |
|---|---|
| Dan Schwanz | Greater Oregon Behavioral Health, Inc. |
| Dr. Judy Shanley | Easterseals |
| Rev. Sally Jo Snyder | Consumer Health Coalition, PA |
| John Sorensen | Centers for Medicare & Medicaid Services; Money Follows the Person |
| Maria Sotnikova | Atlanta Regional Commission |
| Kelsey Walter | National Association of States United for Aging and Disability |
| Jade Warren | Access2Care |
| Eric Weakly | Administration for Community Living |
| Elaine Wells | Ride Connection, Portland, OR |
| Dace West | Mile High Connects |
| Julie Wilcke | Ride Connection, Portland, OR |
| Sally Wilson | Project Access of Durham County, Durham, NC |
| Shirley Wilson | Mississippi DOT |
| Chris Zeilenger | Community Transportation Association of America |

# D

# Biosketches of Speakers and Discussants

**Suzanne Alewine, M.P.A.,** is a Co-Founder and Principal Partner of Community Asset Builders, LLC, in addition to serving as Executive Director of the Missouri Rural Health Association. Community Asset Builders is a health improvement-focused firm providing a variety of services to a diverse array of nonprofit clients that includes federally qualified health centers, hospitals, local public health agencies and statewide associations. Team members provide technical assistance to identify tools and resources to design and sustain community and organizational processes and interventions, develop effective communication strategies, evaluate programs and services, and utilize technology for effective change and cost efficiency. The Missouri Rural Health Association is the administrator of HealthTran, a pilot program linking health care coordination and transportation mobility management services to create a simple, effective approach to improving access to care. HealthTran is currently funded by the Missouri Foundation for Health and the Missouri Department of Transportation through Federal Transit Authority Section 5310 funding.

Ms. Alewine holds an undergraduate degree in Business Administration and a Master's in Public Administration from the University of Missouri. She is a founding member of the Association for Community Health Improvement, is a past co-chair of the national Healthy Communities Network, and a graduate of the Health Forum's Creating Healthier Communities Fellowship.

**Sarah Anderson,** Senior Associate at Cambridge Systematics, currently serves as the Business Development Manager for the Software Business line where she oversees strategic planning, and development of client and partner relationships. Ms. Anderson is an advocate for expanded use of open data and open-source technologies in the public transportation industry and is passionate about technology's role in driving better results for transportation providers and consumers. For the past several years, Ms. Anderson has helped Cambridge grow its presence in the field of mobility management. In particular, finding grant funding and teaming partners for the development and implementation of 1-Click, an open-source, multimodal trip planning and trip booking software.

**Xavier Arinez, M.S.,** graduated summa cum laude with a Bachelor of Science in Mechanical Engineering from the University of Kansas and a Master of Science from the University of Illinois. His professional experience started as a Project Engineer at General Motors in Detroit, Michigan. After 2 years in the automotive industry, Mr. Arinez took three major assignments in South America for American companies expanding into the countries in Bolivia, Colombia, and Brazil, assuming senior engineering and administrative responsibilities for manufacturing plants at the start-up level geared to rapid-growth business models. After 20 years in these roles, his assignments led to the logistics of health care industry where, for the past 6 years, he has acquired a broad experience in practice management and operations in large federally qualified health centers (120,000 visits per year), with emphasis in providing comprehensive health care to underserved populations.

**Anneta Arno, Ph.D., M.P.H.,** is an experienced public health professional with a track record in the field of health equity. This includes national recognition for work promoting community collaboration to transform views and perspectives related to root causes of health disparities, the integration of health equity concepts into health care delivery systems, and racial equity through a public health lens. Prior to joining the team at the District of Columbia Department of Health (DOH), Dr. Arno served as the Division Manager for Communicable Disease Prevention & Public Health Preparedness in the Kansas City, Missouri, Department of Health. She has also served as the Director for the Center for Health Equity in the Louisville Metro Department of Public Health and Wellness and as Adjunct Faculty in the University of Louisville, School of Public Health and Information Sciences. Dr. Arno holds a Ph.D. in Urban Planning and an M.P.H. in Health Care Management.

Dr. Arno's diverse career experiences in public health, philanthropy, urban planning, and academia as well as her spirit of collaboration, make her the ideal candidate to lead the newly minted DOH Office of Health Equity and serve as a critical ambassador for a "health in all policies" approach to improving population health.

**Barry Barker, M.P.A.,** was the 2012 recipient of the prestigious Sharon D. Banks Award for Humanitarian Leadership in Transportation from the Transportation Research Board. He has been honored by Paralyzed Veterans of America, Easterseals, and the NAACP for work advancing workplace diversity and accessible transportation and by the American Public Transportation Association as a top transportation manager. Long active in national, state, and local public service organizations, Mr. Barker is a former Executive Committee member of the American Public Transit Association (APTA) and currently chairs APTA's Legislative Committee. Under his leadership, TARC recognitions include awards for Labor Management, Education-Friendly Employer of the Year, and Psychologically Healthy Workplace. Mr. Barker holds a B.S. in Engineering from Case Western Reserve University and an M.P.A. from Cleveland State University.

**Christopher Barnett, M.A.,** co-directs the Center for Applied Research and Environmental Systems (CARES) at the University of Missouri. Mr. Barnett has been with CARES since 1992, and has worked extensively with geographic information technologies (GITs). His early work combining GIT and Internet technologies contributed to the development of the CARES Map Room and a variety of Web-based information and assessment tools, including the Missouri Clipper, an agricultural management data resource, and the Missouri Comprehensive Community Needs Assessment website. His current interests focus on the practical application of data and tools in an Internet environment.

Mr. Barnett, a native of Missouri, received his B.A. in Geography in 1990 and an M.A. in Geography in 1992, both at the University of Missouri. He is also a member of the Missouri Board on Geographic Names.

**Clyde J. Behney, M.B.A.,** is the Executive Director of the Health and Medicine Division (HMD) of the National Academies of Sciences, Engineering, and Medicine. Previously he concurrently served as the Interim Leonard D. Schaeffer Executive Officer of the National Academy of Medicine. From 1998 until 2013 he was the Deputy Executive Officer of the Institute of Medicine (IOM), overseeing IOM's peer-review process, communications activities, and other activities related to the quality of IOM reports.

Prior to joining the National Academies, he was Assistant Director of the Congressional Office of Technology Assessment (OTA) and Director of the OTA division responsible for health, life sciences, the environment, and education and human resources (1993–1996). From 1981 until 1993, he was the director of OTA's Health Program. Mr. Behney was the co-founder and, from 1981 until its end in 1985, executive director of the Sorcerer's Apprentice Network and editor of its newsletter. He has served as a peer reviewer for *Health Affairs*, the *Milbank Quarterly*, *Medical Care*, *Health*

*Services Research*, and the *American Journal of Public Health*. He received his B.S. from Lehigh University and his M.B.A. from the University of Maryland. He completed all requirements short of the dissertation for his Doctorate in Health Policy at George Washington University. He will never write that dissertation.

**Julie Bershadsky, Ph.D.,** is a Senior Research Specialist at the Human Services Research Institute (HSRI). She is the Director of the National Core Indicators-Aging and Disabilities (NCI-AD) project for HSRI. She is also the primary methodologist, data analyst, and researcher for the National Core Indicators (NCI) (an effort to develop indicators and benchmarks of performance across 45 states' developmental disabilities service systems) and related projects. She works extensively with the NCI data, manages the multi-state dataset, and advises on all methodological issues related to data collection and analysis. Dr. Bershadsky has also provided analytic and methodological guidance and expertise to numerous resource allocation projects that state intellectual and developmental disabilities systems in the United States have undertaken in the recent decade. Dr. Bershadsky's training and experience is as a health services researcher, statistician, and data analyst and is coupled with extensive knowledge of the field of developmental disabilities and aging. She received her Doctorate in Health Services Research and Policy and her B.A. in Statistics from the University of Minnesota, Twin Cities.

**Mary Tonore Blumberg, M.S.,** is the Program Manager for Strategic Planning and Development at the Atlanta Regional Commission (ARC), Aging and Health Resources Division. ARC serves as the planning, development and intergovernmental coordination agency for the 10-county Atlanta region. ARC's purpose is to serve the citizens, local governments, and the broader regional community by providing services, support, and leadership on issues that require comprehensive regional solutions. ARC is designated as both the Atlanta region's Metropolitan Planning Organization (MPO) and Area Agency on Aging (AAA). Ms. Blumberg is responsible for overseeing activities within ARC's Lifelong Community Initiative, which promotes diverse housing and transportation options, opportunities for healthy living, and convenient access to basic services. In addition, she oversees strategic planning for the division, which includes the Area Plan on Aging. She oversees a diversity of transportation programs for older adults, persons with disabilities, and low-income people including Federal Transit Administration 5310, DeKalb County Coordinated Transportation System, and Title III Older American Act transportation services. She previously worked at the Louisiana Governor's Office of Elderly Affairs serving as the Director of Home- and Community-Based Services. She has a B.S. and an M.S. from Louisiana State University in Nutrition and is a Registered Dietitian.

**Charles Carr, M.S.,** is the Director of the Office of Intermodal Planning, which encompasses the Mississippi Department of Transportation's (MDOT's) Freight Waterways, Aeronautics, and Transit divisions. Mr. Carr has more than 35 years of experience in the public sector, including health planning, housing, disaster recovery assistance, and community development. He has more than 25 years of experience in the transportation field, including executive management, policy development, planning, project development, performance evaluation, compliance reviews, and technical assistance. Most recently as the director of the Public Transit Division, he was responsible for policy development, contract management and grants administration for all the public transit programs administered through MDOT. He earned a bachelor's degree in History and Political Science and a master's degree in Sociology/Community Program Development from Jackson State University.

**Flora M. Castillo** is a Vice President of Community and Strategic Engagement at UnitedHealthcare Community & State. She has more than 20 years of health care and managed care experience, specializing in marketing, public relations, communications, advocacy, and business development. Ms. Castillo previously served as Vice President of Marketing and Business Growth at PerformCare, a member of the AmeriHealth Caritas Family of Companies, which is a national full-service managed behavioral health care organization that supports members and providers through specialized behavioral health and human services programs in both the public and private sectors. Ms. Castillo has been a Director of the New Jersey Transit Corporation since 1999 and currently chairs its Customer Service committee. She is also a past Chairwoman of the American Public Transportation Association. A passionate transportation advocate, Ms. Castillo is also a member of the board of the Women's Transportation Seminar based in Washington, DC, the Alan M. Voorhees Transportation Center Advisory Board at Rutgers University, and the Transportation Diversity Council (TDC).

**Raka Choudhury, M.C.R.P.,** is currently Citywide Transportation Planner with the Progressive Transportation Service Administration (PTSA) at the District (of Columbia) Department of Transportation (DDOT). In this position, in addition to managing the TransportDC program, she works with coordinating station area plans, Metrobus studies, and other planning studies with the Washington Metropolitan Area Transportation Authority. Ms.

Choudhury is also DDOT's representative on the National Capital Region Transportation Planning Board's Access for All Advisory Committee. Ms. Choudhury came to DDOT in 2015 with almost 15 years' experience in urban planning and transportation in both the public and private sectors. While the majority of her work has been in the Washington, DC, area, she has also worked in land use and transportation coordination, infrastructure development, and urban policy in South and South East Asia. While she was working in India in 2011–2012, Ms. Choudhury was also an op-ed contributor to *The Wall Street Journal*, writing about planning and transportation issues. Ms. Choudhury has a bachelor's degree in Architecture from the School of Planning and Architecture in New Delhi, India, and a master's degree in City and Regional Planning from The Ohio State University. She has been a certified planner with the American Planning Association since 2007.

**Ed Christopher, M.S.,** has been involved in urban transportation planning since 1979. He has a master's degree in Urban Planning and Policy from the University of Illinois at Chicago with a transportation specialization. Mr. Christopher began his career at the Chicago Area Transportation Study (CATS) in 1979 as the Director of Information Systems. There he was responsible for the collection, acquisition, maintenance, and analysis of the data to support the many activities of CATS, the Metropolitan Planning Organization for the Chicago region. In 1998, Mr. Christopher went to work for the federal government, first at the U.S. Department of Transportation's Bureau of Transportation Statistics (BTS). Between 2001 and December 2015, he was the Metropolitan Planning Specialist for the Federal Highway Administration's Resource Center. In December 2015, Mr. Christopher retired from federal service and has been doing transportation consulting ever since. Mr. Christopher's active work in the field of transportation planning includes working on several transportation and health-related projects, chairing a Transportation Research Board (TRB) Task Force on Arterial Health, co-chairing a TRB sub-committee on health and transportation, and speaking as a national expert at various conferences and workshops on the relationship of health and transportation. Mr. Christopher is also an active member on the TRB National Data Committee as well as the founding chair of a TRB Sub Committee on Census Data for Transportation Planning. He serves as a member at large to the TRB Data Section and is an emeritus member of the urban data committee. Mr. Christopher has a long list of accomplishments and is well known among the transportation planning and data community especially for his work with large datasets, travel behavior research, urban and statewide planning and programming, travel demand forecasting, traffic operations, and travel demand management, as well as developing long-range transportation plans, communicating technical concepts to the public, developing large-scale research projects, and policy analysis and planning.

**Amy Conrick, M.Phil.,** has 16 years' experience in the transportation field, with 16 years as a writer and 10 years as presenter, trainer, facilitator, and program manager in the mobility management and employment transportation fields. Ms. Conrick has provided technical assistance in developing transportation services and related solutions to several communities. She has also facilitated five communities in developing innovative transportation solutions to health care and jobs using a human-centered design approach, and applies portions of this approach to all of her work.

Ms. Conrick has brought her wide-ranging transportation knowledge into the development and delivery of in-person and online trainings. She has planned and facilitated many mobility management, transportation coordination, and team meetings, and has presented on these topics in workshops and conferences as well as on webinars. She has also written and edited educational materials on employment-related and other transportation issues, provided direct technical support to communities and individuals, and developed community and agency self-assessment tools that lead to increased collaboration between the transit community and human service and workforce development agencies.

Ms. Conrick holds an M.Phil. degree in English and Irish Literature from the University College, Dublin, Ireland, and an honors B.A. degree in English Literature from Georgetown University.

**Joe Cronin, Ph.D.,** has held The John R. Kerr Eminent Scholar Chair in Marketing and Service Innovation at Florida State University (FSU) since 2008. Prior to that, he held the Carl DeSantis Professorship in Marketing (2002–2008). He received his Ph.D. in Marketing and Logistics from The Ohio State University. Dr. Cronin is recognized worldwide as a leading service marketing scholar, particularly in the conceptualization and measurement of service quality, service value, and customer satisfaction. The citations of his articles currently exceed 25,600. His co-authored 1992 *Journal of Marketing* article related to the measurement of service quality has been noted as the second most cited of all articles published in the *Journal of Marketing* over the past 25 years. Two other *Journal of Marketing* articles (1994 and 2001) are also highly cited, and a fourth was recently accepted (2016). A 2000 article he co-authored that contrast the effects of service quality, service value, and customer satisfaction is currently listed as the fifth most frequently downloaded *Journal of Retailing* article. A 2005 *Journal of Retailing* article that extends this research is also among the journals most frequently downloaded papers. A 2009 co-authored *Journal* *of Service Research* article was runner-up for the journal's annual Best Article Award.

Dr. Cronin's research has also been published the *Journal of the Academy of Marketing Science*, the *Journal of Services Research*, the *Strategic Management Journal*, the *European Journal of Marketing*, the *Journal of Advertising*, the *International Journal of Operations & Production Management*, and other marketing journals. He currently serves as an Associate Editor of the *Journal of Services Marketing* and the *Journal of Business Research*. Dr. Cronin currently serves, or has served, on the editorial review boards of the *Journal of Marketing*, the *Journal of the Academy of Marketing Science*, the *Journal of Retailing*, the *Journal of Services Research*, the *Journal of Service Management*, the *Journal of Business Research*, *Managing Service Quality*, *Health Marketing Quarterly*, and the *Journal of Management Research*. Dr. Cronin has chaired 17 dissertations at FSU placing his graduates at such schools as Cornell, Michigan State, Boston College, Auburn, and Texas Tech. Dr. Cronin has also been the recipient of an FSU University Undergraduate Teaching Award.

**Marcie Cynamon** is Director of the National Health Interview Survey (NHIS), a large general purpose health survey of the civilian, noninstitutionalized U.S. population. The NHIS is a primary source of data on health care coverage, health status, health behaviors, and access to health care conducted by the National Center for Health Statistics. Her expertise is in health survey methods research and launching new surveys.

**Moumita Dasgupta, Ph.D.**, is the Director of Smart Transit for Healthcare and holds a teaching position at Amherst College. She completed her Ph.D. in Experimental Physics from Clark University, Worcester, Massachusetts, in 2015. Her endeavor, Smart Transit for Healthcare, developed a software interface prototype that facilitates scheduling of a patient's appointment at a hospital by taking care of his or her transportation needs, especially for patients from low-income brackets. Smart Transit collaborates with Cambridge Systematics for development and refinement of the software solution to better align with One Click platform, the open-source multimodal trip planner. Right now Smart Transit is collaborating with Jacksonville Transportation Authority, Florida, Pennsylvania Department of Transportation, and Pioneer Valley Transit Authority, Massachusetts, to share their learnings and different relevant aspects of their software solution to tailor these agencies to lead to a solution that meets the needs of patients in their area based on the same model.

**Virginia L. Dize, M.S.**, is Co-Director of the National Aging and Disability Transportation Center (NADTC)/Program Manager, National Association of Area Agencies on Aging (n4a). Ms. Dize has more than 30 years' experience in aging programs and joined the staff of n4a in 2008. She managed several rounds of demonstration grants under the National Center on Senior Transportation (NCST), which she co-directed from 2008 through 2015, and has done work on older driver safety, pedestrian safety, volunteer driver programs, transportation for elders living on Native American reservations, and diversity. In addition, she oversees n4a's efforts to support transportation within the aging network and related transportation projects. She developed the Inclusive Coordinated Transportation Partnership project's grant program, funded by the Administration for Community Living (ACL), as well as guidance on call center operations under the Federal Transit Administration's Veterans Transportation Community Living Initiative. She has a Master of Science degree in Gerontology from Virginia Commonwealth University (1982) and is the author of publications on senior transportation, consumer direction, long-term care, and elder rights.

**David N. Faldmo, M.P.A.S., PA-C,** is the Medical Director of Siouxland Community Health Center (SCHC). Mr. Faldmo, who has been at SCHC since 1993, received his medical training at the Roy J. and Lucille A. Carver College of Medicine, University of Iowa.

Mr. Faldmo completed a Community Health Center Executive Fellowship through University of Kansas Medical Center.

**Carolyn Flowers, M.B.A.,** is currently the Acting Administrator of the Federal Transit Administration (FTA). She joined FTA as Senior Advisor in January 2015 and was appointed FTA Deputy Administrator on April 18, 2016. In this role, Ms. Flowers will be carrying out the functions and duties of the position of Administrator. Ms. Flowers leads a staff of more than 500 in the Washington, DC, headquarters office and 10 regional offices throughout the United States, and implements an annual budget of more than $10 billion. Ms. Flowers' decades-long career serving in public transit provides FTA invaluable insight and guidance for delivering its programs, policies, and initiatives. Prior to joining FTA, Ms. Flowers served as Chief Executive Officer/Director of Public Transit for the Charlotte Area Transit System, where she was responsible for countywide bus and rail transit planning and management. She began her career in public transportation with the Los Angeles County Metropolitan Transportation Authority (LACMTA) in 1993 and for 19 years served in many capacities in budget, administration, and operations at LACMTA. Her last position at LACMTA was as the Chief Operations Officer with responsibility for managing bus operations and Freeway Service Patrol. Ms. Flowers earned a bachelor's degree in History and Political Science and a master's degree in Business Administration from the University of California, Los Angeles (UCLA), School of

Management. She has served on a number of professional boards, including co-chairing the American Public Transportation Association's (APTA's) Reauthorization Task Force, and has received a number of awards for her commitment to advancing public transportation nationwide. She participated in a 2005 international study project for the National Association of Sciences, sponsored by the Eno Foundation for Transportation Studies, as well as the executive development program sponsored by the Eno Center for Transit Leadership.

**Richard Garrity** is a Senior Associate with RLS & Associates, Inc., and is based in the Wilmington, North Carolina, area. He brings more than 31 years of progressive experience in transit and paratransit planning, operations and management evaluation, policy development, and state department of transportation (DOT) program management of Federal Transit Administration (FTA) programs. Mr. Garrity specializes in federal regulatory issues, including charter, interstate transportation, and ADA/paratransit operations issues, and is a highly regarded trainer for community transportation programs. Mr. Garrity's combination of state DOT experience combined with his many years of consulting work with the federal government as well as state and local governments and all sizes of transit systems make him uniquely qualified on a number of subjects, but in particular financial management and oversight and regulatory compliance.

**Oscar C. Gomez** is the Chief Executive Officer of Health Outreach Partners (HOP). Originally from south Los Angeles, Mr. Gomez was born to Mexican immigrants and is bilingual in English and Spanish. Mr. Gomez holds a B.A. in International Studies from Pepperdine University and has more than 23 years of experience in the field of community health. He joined HOP (then East Coast Migrant Health Project) in 1992 as an Administrative Assistant and dedicated himself to HOP's work, eventually being named CEO in July 2000. As HOP's CEO, he has led HOP through two company redesigns including a scope expansion from a regional service area to a national scope and focus on safety net organizations that serve low-income, marginalized, and vulnerable communities. He also served as a member of the National Seasonal & Migrant Head Start Advisory Council and as Board Treasurer for the California Institute on Rural Studies. In 2008 he received a certificate from the University of California, Los Angeles, Anderson School of Management for completion of their Health Care Executive Program and is a former LeaderSpring Executive Fellow, focusing on equity, social justice, and social change. Mr. Gomez has served on numerous community and national board of directors addressing issues related to community health, migrant health, education, and public health research. In addition to professional experience and educational opportunities, Mr. Gomez strongly believes that his interpersonal skills and intercultural perspective are rooted in his extensive personal travel throughout the globe, including Cuba, the Middle East, New Zealand, and rural America.

**Roy Grant, M.A.,** is a public health research consultant based in New York City. Following 3 years on the editorial board of *American Journal of Public Health* (*AJPH*), he is now a Department Editor for *AJPH*. Previously, Mr. Grant was Research Director at the Children's Health Fund for 15 years and directed community pediatric programs for Mount Sinai Medical Center for 10 years. Mr. Grant has published more than four dozen book chapters and papers in peer-reviewed journals, including *New England Journal of Medicine*, *JAMA Pediatrics*, *Pediatrics*, *AJPH*, *Maternal & Child Health Journal*, and many others. In addition to his area of clinical specialty, early childhood mental health and development, Mr. Grant has published on diverse topics including transportation and health care access, service needs of vulnerable populations, cost savings of clinical best practices, integrated primary and behavioral health care, and the interface between public health research and public policy.

**Yahaira Graxirena, M.A.,** is a Principal Transportation Planner for the Central Massachusetts Regional Planning Commission, an entity that supports the Central Mass MPO 40-member communities and acts as the planning arm of the Worcester Regional Transit Authority (WRTA). Mrs. Graxirena worked on the Automatic Data Collection System implementation for the WRTA, assisted in the calibration/validation of the APC data and its subsequent certification process. Her roles included route planning, and development of performance metrics and support systems to operational decisions as a way to increase accessibility to basic needs and services within the WRTA service area. As the agency's Title VI/Environmental Justice (EJ) liaison, she had collaborated with numerous local organizations within the Central Mass region, most recently through the Mobility2040, the region's long-range transportation plan. Currently, Mrs. Graxirena is part of the Federal Highway Administration's core group for the EJ Tools Peer Network. She has worked closely with the Worcester Division of Public Health in the development of the Greater Worcester Community Health Improvement Plan (CHIP) and recently was appointed to serve in the local Community Health Network Area (CHNA) Steering Committee, charged with implementing the CHIP. At the state level, she was appointed in 2014 to be part of the Massachusetts Healthy Transportation Compact Advisory Council as the state's strategy to achieve positive health outcomes through the coordination of transportation, land use, and public health policy. Also, she was part of the Worcester's Food and Active Living Policy Council Steering Committee from 2012 to 2015. Last year, she became the team leader on the development of the Healthcare Access Mobility Design challenge grant, a Ladders of Opportunity initiative from the National Center for Mobility Management and the Community Transportation Association of America to explore solutions to improve access to the Family Health Center in Worcester using a design-thinking approach. Currently her tasks include the development of performance measures and multimodal analyses related to the Vision Zero goal as an effort to reduce fatalities and serious injuries in the region's roadway system, and to expand the Central Massachusetts Metropolitan Planning Organization data integration program.

Mrs. Graxirena, born and raised in Puerto Rico, holds a B.A. in Environmental Design from the School of Architecture and an M.A. in Planning, both from the University of Puerto Rico. She is a member of the Conference of Minority Transportation Officials, Boston Chapter.

**Heidi Guenin, Ph.D.**, is a Senior Associate with GridWorks in Portland, Oregon. Prior to joining GridWorks, she worked with Upstream Public Health as the Transportation and Land Use Policy Manager. She has more than 10 years of experience working with community members, government staff, and elected decision makers, and researching, developing, and advocating for transportation and land use policies to reduce health disparities. Dr. Guenin completed her bachelor of arts in Economics and English Language and Literature at the University of Virginia, a master of public health at Oregon Health & Science University, and a master of urban and regional planning at Portland State University.

**Art Guzzetti, M.P.A.**, a 33-year veteran of public transportation at the local, state, and national levels, serves as Vice President-Policy for the American Public Transportation Association (APTA), the trade group representing the public transportation industry in the United States. Among other things, Mr. Guzzetti is responsible for APTA's extensive policy research agenda, policy analysis and development, and transportation information and statistics. Mr. Guzzetti and the APTA team work with legislative and executive branches of all levels of government, and with other national associations, think tanks, and interest groups to cultivate the ideas, relationships, and advocacy initiatives that will propel public transportation forward.

Prior to coming to APTA in June 1997, Mr. Guzzetti had 16 years in management at two of the nation's leading public transportation systems: New Jersey Transit, and Port Authority of Allegheny County, plus 2 years at the New Jersey Department of Transportation. His duties focused on transportation policy, government affairs, capital programming, grants development, and grants management and advocacy. In short, his career focus has been on generating support for public transportation and the benefits it provides to communities and regions.

Mr. Guzzetti has a Political Science degree from Edinboro State University, and a Master of Public Administration degree from the University of Pittsburgh.

**Paul Hughes-Cromwick, M.A.**, is a Senior Health Economist at Altarum Institute, where he has worked since 2002. He has been involved in health care economic and policy analyses since receiving his master's degree in 1981. He leads outreach activities for the Center for Sustainable Health Spending, which was launched by Altarum as a critical systems issue in May 2011.

Before working at Altarum, Mr. Hughes-Cromwick worked for the University of Michigan School of Nursing; the Henry Ford Health System; the University of Pittsburgh Graduate School of Public Health; the State of Connecticut, where he was Research Director for the Connecticut Partnership for Long-Term Care Insurance; and the U.S. Department of Health and Human Services in the Office of the Assistant Secretary for Planning and Evaluation. He was chairman of the board at Care Choices HMO in Farmington Hills, Michigan, until its sale, and is currently on the board of trustees of Health Alliance Plan in Detroit, Michigan. He is a member of the American Economic Association; AcademyHealth; the American Public Health Association; and the National Association for Business Economics, where he serves as chairman of the Health Economics Roundtable. Mr. Hughes-Cromwick has a B.S. in Mathematics and Philosophy from the University of Notre Dame and an M.A. in Applied Economics from Clark University, where he completed all nondissertation requirements toward a Ph.D. His areas of expertise include health economics, health policy analysis and forecasting, and health sector economic indicators.

**Dennis Johnson, M.P.M.**, is Executive Vice President for Policy, Advocacy, and Government Affairs at the Children's Health Fund, a nonprofit organization that initiates and supports innovative pediatric programs designed to meet the complex health care needs of medically underserved, homeless, and economically disadvantaged children. Mr. Johnson is also the Policy Director, National Center for Disaster Preparedness at Columbia University's Earth Institute, where he acts as a liaison between the center and policymakers and elected officials at the state and federal levels.

Mr. Johnson directs the Fund's public policy, government affairs, and advocacy agendas and coordinates the Fund's relationship with a broad spectrum of public officials, public- and private-sector entities, advocacy groups, and health provider organizations.

Prior to his current position, Mr. Johnson was Vice President of External Affairs and Senior Director, Policy and Planning. Before that, he served as the Interim Director of the Fund's national network of mobile-based pediatric programs.

Prior to his tenure at the Children's Health Fund, Mr. Johnson was a Senior Program Officer at the Fund for New York City Public Education and a Research Analyst at the Public Policy Institute of the Business Council of New York State.

Mr. Johnson received his bachelor's degree from the University of Pennsylvania and his master's degree in Political Management from the Graduate School of Political Management at Baruch College.

**Judy Kell** has been Hub Manager of Pathways to Better Health of the Lakeshore, part of Muskegon Community Health Project, since 2012. Her role includes managing a Centers for Medicare & Medicaid Services innovation project to deploy community health workers to assist individuals with two or more chronic diseases who have or are eligible for Medicaid and Medicare to address social determinants of care. Ms. Kell was previously Chief Operating Officer of West Michigan Therapy after 4 years of serving as Grant Coordinator for the County of Muskegon. Ms. Kell has more than two decades of experience in strategic planning, grant writing, and program evaluation services to hospitals, coordinating agencies for substance abuse services, Michigan Department of Corrections, nursing homes, and governmental and nonprofit agencies.

**Katherine Kortum, Ph.D.**, is a Senior Program Officer at the Transportation Research Board where she creates and guides committees analyzing transportation policy topics, such as regulation of new mobility options (including Uber and Lyft), transit asset management, development of federal research plans, and intercity passenger travel. In 2015–2016, she was also a Robert Bosch Fellow, working with the Innovationszentrum für Mobilität und gesellschaftlichen Wandel GmbH (InnoZ) in Berlin, on shared and integrated mobility research projects. She was elected chair of Young Professionals in Transportation by the international membership 3 years in a row and managed the nonprofit professional organization. Dr. Kortum was also appointed chair of the Institute of Transportation Engineer's Younger Member Committee in 2013. In addition, she has spoken in a number of settings on the development of the next generation of the transportation workforce and on innovations facing the industry. Dr. Kortum holds an M.S. and a Ph.D. in Transportation Engineering from The University of Texas at Austin and a B.S. in Civil Engineering from the University of Pittsburgh. She is a Professional Engineer in Washington, DC.

**Catherine Lawson, Ph.D.,** is Geography and Planning Associate Professor at the State University of New York at Albany, where she examines Urban transportation data and information systems, hazardous materials transport, transportation and land use connection, and microsimulation and GIS applications. She is currently leading a team of researchers and students in the AVAIL (Albany Visualization And Informatics Lab) project, which seeks to empower a new generation of graduates to assimilate computer science knowledge and subject-matter expertise in the mining and dissemination of "big data," as they create groundbreaking Web-based solutions for government and business. The AVAIL team is tackling a range of open-source and open-data projects. Working with New Jersey Transit, AVAIL is incorporating U.S. Census household data into microsimulations of bus transit ridership to provide travelers with ultra-efficient open-source trip-planning. Dr. Lawson's team is also developing a Cloud-based decision support system for New York's Mesonet, a statewide network of automated weather stations. Through an AVAIL-produced interactive Web-based map, Mesonet stakeholders will select evidence-based sites that best serve New York. Overseas, AVAIL is transforming an academic study on community gardens by University of Glasgow colleagues into an interactive map to increase community participation in agriculture network expansion.

**Valerie Lefler, M.P.A.,** is President and CEO of Liberty Mobility Now, Inc. Ms. Lefler has a degree in Business Administration from the University of Nebraska–Lincoln and a master's degree in Public Administration from the University of Nebraska–Omaha. Ms. Lefler spent almost 12 years in managing university transportation research and then transitioned to specializing in rural public transportation regulation and public outreach. Based on that experience, Ms. Lefler started her own business and submitted a Small Business Innovative Research (SBIR) project to the U.S. Department of Transportation Federal Transit Administration to use advanced technology to design customer-focused mobility options—called Liberty. The project has now evolved into a formal company dedicated to providing responsive customer-centered care across the United States.

**Ysela Llort** is the past Director of Miami-Dade Transit (MDT). She was appointed to this position by Mayor Carlos A. Gimenez in February 2012. From August 2011 to February 2012, she served as MDT's Interim Director. Prior to being at the helm of MDT, Ms. Llort served as an Assistant County Manager, responsible for the county's major transportation departments, which included MDT, Public Works, Miami-Dade Aviation, and Seaport (Port of Miami), as well as the County's Consumer Services Department. Ms. Llort also was responsible for overseeing the Citizens' Independent Transportation Trust and the Metropolitan Planning Organization.

Before working for Miami-Dade County, Ms. Llort was the Florida Department of Transportation's Assistant Secretary for Intermodal Systems Development; she was responsible for the executive management and operation of the department's planning, environmental management and public transportation programs. Ms. Llort directed the long range and strategic planning and formulation of policy for developing capital improvement and investment plans for the state's intermodal transportation facilities

**Ann Lundy, M.B.A., B.S.N.,** is the Vice President, Medical Management at Health Care Service Corporation. She is a dynamic health care professional with more than 25 years of experience in leading, designing, managing, structuring, and implementing operational policies and procedures that support business for Medicaid and Dual Medicare managed care programs. She has identified strategies in developing programs, across multiple business lines, to achieve mission, goals, and objectives. Ms. Lundy, nationally led the development, implementation and outcome measurement of the clinical Utilization Management, Case Management, Population Health, Disease Management programs for Medicaid including all populations of Aged, Blind, and Disabled (ABD), Temporary Assistance for Needy Families (TANF), Children's Health Insurance Program (CHIP), Long-Term Services and Supports (LTSS), Intellectual Disabilities/Development Disabilities (ID/DD), and Complex Care, Long-Term Care Medicaid and Dual Special Needs populations in multiple states. Ms. Lundy is a registered nurse with a bachelor's degree from Indiana University and has a Master's of Business Administration from Rockhurst University. She has served on multiple boards and volunteers on a regular basis at several homeless shelters.

**Jana Lynott** manages AARP's transportation research agenda and is responsible for the development of policy related to transportation and other livable communities issues adopted by the AARP Policy Council and Board of Directors and presented in the AARP Policy Book. Her research focuses on human services transportation coordination, accessible street design, the travel patterns of older adults, transit service needs, and older driver safety.

Ms. Lynott was responsible for the development of AARP's Livability Index, which was released in April 2015. This first-of-its-kind online tool blends mapping technology, preference survey results, quantitative measures, and public policies to measure how well a location—down to the neighborhood level—is meeting residents' current and future needs. It uses a scoring system of 60 indicators spread across seven categories of livability: housing, neighborhood, transportation, environment, health, engagement, and opportunity.

Before her employment with AARP, Ms. Lynott was Director of Transportation Planning for the Northern Virginia Transportation Commission, where she designed and managed a groundbreaking study on the link between land use and the mobility of older adults. She also initiated and managed a travel instruction program to teach seniors how to use transit services. As a land use and transportation planner, Ms. Lynott brings practical expertise to the research field.

**Heather MacLeod** is an Assistant Director at the U.S. Government Accountability Office (GAO). She has extensive experience in the design and execution of research and analysis resulting in studies presented to the U.S. Congress. Ms. MacLeod has led numerous teams and studies related to surface transportation, aviation, and other issues. Ms. MacLeod is based in GAO's Seattle Field Office and assigned to GAO's Physical Infrastructure team.

**Peter McNichol** is Medicaid NEMT Quality Control Chief at the Department of Vermont Health Access. Mr. McNichol has been working with the Vermont Medicaid program for 15 years, and has been working specifically with Vermont's nonemergency medical transportation (NEMT) program since 2006. As Quality Control Chief for the Department of Vermont Health Access, his department oversees Vermont's contracted system of public transportation brokers. This oversight includes, but is not limited to, program audits, member eligibility, compliance, and program quality control.

Mr. McNichol is currently serving as a panel member with the Transit Cooperative Research Program's research project TCRP B-44, Impact of the Trend Toward Separate Statewide Medicaid Transportation Brokerages on Human Services Transportation Coordination.

**Perry Meadows, M.D.,** is Medical Director, Government Programs, for Geisinger Health Plan. He is the medical lead for government programs, which includes Medicare and Medicaid. His responsibilities include health care services and the development of medical necessity guidelines for Geisinger Health Plan. He is also the medical director lead for Geisinger Health Plan Fraud, Waste, and Abuse.

Dr. Meadows has been with Geisinger Health Plan since August 2014. Prior to joining Geisinger Health Plan, he was in Louisville, Kentucky, for several years.

Dr. Meadows graduated from Marshall University with a Bachelor of Science in Chemistry, a Master of Science in Biological Sciences, and a Doctorate of Medicine. He completed his internship and residency at Marshall University School of Medicine in Family Practice. He is a fellow of the American Academy of Family Practice and is board certified in Family Practice. He also received his Juris Doctor from Salmon P. Chase College of Law, Northern Kentucky University, and his M.B.A. from Regis University.

**Alex Page, M.C.R.P.,** is the lead Service Planner for Ride Connection in Portland, Oregon. His projects focus on last-mile connections to regional transit, community connector shuttles for areas with limited transit services, and demand-response transportation programs targeted for seniors and people with disabilities. He specializes in implementing flexible transit services that blend demand-response and fixed-route models. He holds a Master of Community and Regional Planning from the University of Oregon. Mr. Page is an active transit, bicycle, and pedestrian advocate to promote public health and increase quality of life in our communities.

**Neil Pedersen** is Executive Director of the Transportation Research Board (TRB) of the National Academies of Sciences, Engineering, and Medicine. Mr. Pedersen joined the National Academies in 2012 as the Deputy Director of the second Strategic Highway Research Program (SHRP 2) after more than 36 years of experience in the transportation profession. For 29 years Mr. Pedersen served in management and leadership positions at the Maryland Department of Transportation's State Highway Administration (SHA), including as Chief Executive Officer for more than 8 years.

A native of Massachusetts, Mr. Pedersen earned bachelor's degrees in Civil Engineering and Urban Studies from Bucknell University and a master's degree in Civil Engineering from Northwestern University. He began his career as a consultant in transportation planning, working first for R.H. Pratt Associates and then for JHK and Associates. He managed projects ranging from travel demand forecasting to transit alternatives analyses and toll road feasibility studies.

In December 1982 he joined SHA as Deputy Director of the Office of Planning and Preliminary Engineering; in 1984 he became Director of that office. Mr. Pedersen served in that post until July 2000, when he was appointed Deputy Administrator for Planning and Engineering, with responsibility for SHA's planning, environmental, engineering, and real estate activities. In January 2003 Mr. Pedersen was named Administrator of SHA. In this role he served as principal adviser to the Governor and the Secretary of Transportation on highway-related matters and provided strategic leadership to an agency of 3,200 employees who plan, design, construct, maintain, and operate Maryland's 5,200-mile state highway network and 2,500 bridges. Mr. Pedersen also had oversight responsibility for Maryland's highway safety and motor carrier programs, and he led delivery of the state's two megaprojects—the Woodrow Wilson Bridge and the Intercounty Connector. Throughout his tenure, Mr. Pedersen remained technically engaged in the science and art of planning and engineering while providing highly effective management and leadership, often in a politically charged context.

For the American Association of State Highway and Transportation

Officials (AASHTO), Mr. Pedersen served as Chair of the Task Force on Context-Sensitive Solutions, Vice Chair of the Standing Committee on Highways, and Vice Chair of the Subcommittee on Asset Management. He also was a member of AASHTO's Standing Committee on Research, and Standing Committee on Planning.

Before joining the TRB staff, Mr. Pedersen was an active volunteer at TRB for more than 30 years, serving on numerous committees and panels. He is a past chair of the TRB Executive Committee, the Technical Activities Council, and the SHRP 2 Technical Coordinating Committee for Capacity Research. He also served as a member of the Executive Committee's Subcommittee on Planning and Policy Review and the National Cooperative Highway Research Program Project Panel on Research for the AASHTO Standing Committee on Highways. In addition, he is an Emeritus Member of the TRB Committee on Statewide Multimodal Transportation Planning.

Among his honors, Mr. Pedersen has received the George S. Bartlett Award (2006), the Road Gang's Lester P. Lamm Award (2005), the Planner of the Year Award from the Maryland Chapter of the American Planning Association (1997), AASHTO's Intermodal Award (1994), and the Community Service Award of the Institute of Transportation Engineers' Baltimore–Washington Chapter (1992).

**Robin Phillips** joined National Rural Transit Assistance Program (RTAP) in December 2014 with almost 18 years of experience working with Federal Transit Administration programs. Ms. Phillips went to law school after getting a B.A. in history from Reed College in Portland, Oregon, and practiced law for 5 years. She decided that municipal bonds and energy litigation were not connected enough to community development issues to be truly satisfying, so she went on to work for Oregon Department of Transportation, where she was hired to write and implement a multimodal intercity policy. The Oregon Intercity Network was the result. This collaboration between the 5311 program and the rail program shifted the paradigm from community projects to regional connectivity and access to transportation networks.

Parallel to service development was the realization that information about services was as important as the services themselves. In 2005, as Administrator of Coordinated Transportation at Washington State Department of Transportation, Ms. Phillips hired staff to create the simplest data schema possible to run the Google transit trip planner. She then worked on finding ways to help rural providers input their data, to increase awareness and access to services.

Finding the right balance of public and private investment has been integral to Ms. Phillips's career. In Oregon there was little money, and private transportation services needed to stay in business in order to meet access and connectivity goals. The integration of public and private operators into the Oregon and Washington state networks was key to their success. In 2007 Ms. Phillips was hired as Senior Policy Director at the American Bus Association, where she facilitated private operators trying to work with the state and federal programs, and vice versa. Working at National RTAP is a natural culmination of Ms. Phillips's experience and her dedication to improving transportation options in rural communities.

**Michelle Proser, M.P.P.,** is the Director of Research at the National Association of Community Health Centers (NACHC), where she conducts research and writing related to health centers, access to care issues, health disparities, quality improvement and care integration, and other issues related to medically underserved populations. She is responsible for analyzing data from all federally qualified health centers, as well as other data sources. She has authored and co-authored numerous reports, articles, and other publications on community health centers and primary care. Ms. Proser also coordinates activities that promote community-based participatory research as a tool for improving community health. She received her Master's in Public Policy from George Washington University and is currently working on her Doctorate in Public Policy at the same institution.

**Marsha Regenstein, Ph.D.,** is a Professor of Health Policy and Management at George Washington University. She also directs the Milken Institute School of Public Health's Doctor of Public Health Program. Dr. Regenstein is the Director of Research and Evaluation for the National Center for Medical-Legal Partnership and is principal investigator for a Health Research and Services Administration-funded evaluation of the Teaching Health Center program created by the Patient Protection and Affordable Care Act. Along with dozens of other projects, Dr. Regenstein has served in leadership roles in four multi-site quality-improvement initiatives designed to improve the quality and accessibility of health care for low-income and underserved individuals. Previously, she was Vice President of Research for the National Association of Public Hospitals and Health Systems and Vice President of the Economic and Social Research Institute.

**Julia Resnick, M.P.H.,** is a Senior Program Manager with Association for Community Health Improvement (ACHI) and the Health Research & Educational Trust. Ms. Resnick is responsible for day-to-day operations of ACHI as well as developing the educational curriculum, analyzing survey data, and planning the ACHI National Conference. In addition to her ACHI responsibilities, she works on a variety of population health-related projects through the American Hospital Association's Health Research &

Educational Trust, including leading the Population Health Task Force and writing guides for Hospitals in Pursuit of Excellence. She is passionate about fostering a health care system that aims to keep people healthy. Prior to joining ACHI, Ms. Resnick worked as a Research Coordinator on National Institutes of Health–funded grants at NorthShore University HealthSystem. As a volunteer fellow in Israel, she worked in a community clinic and coordinated perinatal care for pregnant African refugee women. Ms. Resnick received her Master of Public Health at Hebrew University's Braun School of Public Health and Community Medicine and a Bachelor of Arts in Sociology from Bates College.

**David Riley, M.S.W.,** is the Director of the Veterans Transportation Program (VTP) in the Veterans Health Administration. VTP consists of Beneficiary Travel (BT), the Highly Rural Transportation Grants Program (HRTGP), and Veterans Transportation Service (VTS).

VTS is a sub-initiative of the Department of Veterans Affairs (VA) initiative, Enhancing Veteran Experience and Access to Healthcare. The program is at more than 100 Veterans Health Administration (VHA) sites and focuses on providing transportation solutions for veterans that increase access to care and overcome barriers that discourage veterans from accessing VHA services. BT is a complex program that provides access to care through travel reimbursement to veterans and payment for some transportation services. BT had national expenditures of more than $850 million in FY15. HRTGP provides grants for Veteran Service Organizations and State Veteran Agencies to improve transportation options for veterans in counties averaging less than seven persons per square mile.

Mr. Riley has been in his current position for 6 years and has 19 years as a VA employee, beginning as a clinical social worker in the Greater Los Angeles Healthcare System. He was the Chief of Social Work Service at the Battle Creek VAMC prior to assuming his current position. He has an M.S.W. from the University of California, Los Angeles, and a B.A. in Communication from the University of Wisconsin.

**Bruce Robinson, M.A.,** is the Acting Associate Administrator for Federal Transit Administration (FTA) Office of Program Management. He has served as the Deputy Associate Administrator for that office since 2012. Along with the Associate Administrator, he oversees the Office of Transit Programs, the Office of Capital Project Management, and the Office of Grants Management and Guidance. Collectively, these offices administer a national program of capital and operating assistance by directing program implementation through FTA regional offices. The office provides procedures and program guidance to assist the field staff and grant recipients in grant program administration and grant management requirements and manages FTA's major project capital oversight programs. Previously he served as the Deputy Associate Administrator for the Office of Research, Demonstration and Innovation. Mr. Robinson joined the Department of Transportation in 1997 within the Office of Acquisition Management of the Federal Highway Administration. He holds a Master of Arts from Yale University and a Bachelor of Arts from the University of North Carolina at Chapel Hill.

**Judy Shanley, Ph.D.**, is the Vice President of Education and Youth Transition at Easterseals, Inc., Chicago, Illinois. She manages projects, provides technical assistance, conducts research, and develops materials regarding accessible transportation, mobility management, and coordinated transportation, and also oversees Easterseals national youth transition programs. Dr. Shanley serves as a project director to several large national centers, funded by the Federal Transit Administration (FTA), and the Administration for Community Living, including the National Center for Mobility Management. She supports FTA in its implementation of national and local Rides to Wellness initiatives. Prior to Easterseals, Dr. Shanley worked at the Department of Education, where she served as a Technical Assistance Chair for United We Ride and has more than 30 years of experience in supporting individuals with disabilities. She earned her Ph.D. in Special Education from the University of Florida and an M.B.A. and a Master's in Rehabilitation Counseling, both from Syracuse University.

**Anson Stewart** is a Ph.D. candidate in the Interdepartmental Doctoral Program in Transportation at the Massachusetts Institute of Technology (MIT). His research, affiliated with the MIT Transit Research Group, the Mobility Futures Collaborative, and the Bus Rapid Transit Center of Excellence, revolves around urban design, open data, accessibility indicators, and civic engagement. His dissertation centers on the value of interactive connectivity mapping tools for communicating with stakeholders about public transit projects.

A native of Southern California, Mr. Stewart is a graduate of Swarthmore College. He has worked with transit agencies, including Los Angeles Metro (Los Angeles, California) and Transantiago (Santiago de Chile), as well as community-based organizations such as Alternatives for Community and Environment (Roxbury, Massachusetts) and municipal governments (Irvine, California). He has participated in transportation planning and design workshops in Chile, China, Colombia, and the United States. As a 2010–2011 Thomas J. Watson Fellow, Mr. Stewart spent 1 year in Latin America and Africa researching emerging bus rapid transit systems and their impacts on incumbent operators and the environment.

**Marianne Stock, M.B.A.,** is currently Division Chief of Rural and Targeted Programs for the Federal Transit Administration (FTA). She is responsible for the administration of FTA formula and discretionary grant programs for rural areas, tribes, and the enhanced mobility of seniors and individuals with disabilities. This includes the management of three technical assistance centers and overseeing FTA's leadership of the Coordinating Council on Access and Mobility.

Ms. Stock came to FTA in 2015 after 32 years with New Jersey Transit, most recently as Program Director, Community Mobility. In that role, Ms. Stock oversaw administration of New Jersey Transit's pass-through grant program for subrecipients, including providing grant support, technical assistance, and compliance oversight to county, municipal, and private nonprofit transit services funded through a variety of state and federal grant programs. Ms. Stock also oversaw planning functions related to data collection and analysis, including travel demand modeling and market research, and developed Title VI equity analysis procedures for New Jersey Transit. She previously directed New Jersey Transit's strategic planning and policy development efforts. Ms. Stock has a B.A. from the University of Virginia and an M.B.A. from New York University's Stern School of Business Administration.

**Steven Strauss, M.B.A.,** is a Deputy Associate Director of the Progressive Transportation Service Administration (PTSA) at the District of Columbia Department of Transportation (DDOT) in Washington, DC. In this position he manages the District's annual capital and operating contributions to the Washington Metropolitan Area Transportation Authority, is responsible for the District's School Transit subsidy program, and serves as the District's Alternate Representative on the Northeast Corridor Commission. Mr. Strauss came to DDOT from New York City (NYC) in June 2008 to join then DDOT Director Emeka Moneme as his Special Assistant. Mr. Strauss began his public sector career at the NYC Office of Management and Budget in 1980, where he was involved with budget oversight of the NYC Department of Transportation. He moved to the Metropolitan Transportation Authority (MTA) in 1982, where he spent 10 years in a variety of increasingly more responsible positions in the budget and planning departments. He was the Special Assistant to the Chief Financial Officer of the MTA, Mortimer Downey, for approximately 3 years. In 1993 Mr. Strauss became an Assistant Director of Government and Community Relations at New York City Transit, an operating subsidiary of the MTA. He managed nearly all of the outreach activities to community groups, neighborhood associations, BIDs, and elected officials for the agency in the borough of Manhattan for 9 years.

Mr. Strauss was born in Little Rock, Arkansas, and began his lifelong interest in transportation and infrastructure opposing the construction of an urban interstate highway during the Earth Day movement of the early 1970s. He attended Dartmouth College in Hanover, New Hampshire, and received a master's degree in Business Administration from Columbia University in New York City.

**Vincent Valdes** was named Federal Transit Administration (FTA) Associate Administrator for Research, Demonstration, and Innovation on April 13, 2016. As Associate Administrator for the Office of Research, Innovation, and Demonstration, Mr. Valdes will be managing an office of 40 program managers, transportation specialists, and engineers who work on FTA's critical transit research program. The program provides research leadership to the transit industry and facilitates the development of transit technologies and techniques that support national transportation goals. Over the past 2 years Mr. Valdes was Director of FTA's Office of Oversight and Program Guidance. Under his leadership, the Oversight office has been extensively revamped in order to streamline and improve productivity, performance, and efficiency. As a result of these efforts, the oversight program has achieved a 20 percent increase in oversight reviews and an ability to anticipate problems among grantees before they become major issues. In his 25 years as a senior manager in the public and private sectors—the last 6 with FTA—Mr. Valdes has demonstrated a clear ability to lead change and innovation in transportation research, urban and regional planning, engineering research, neighborhood economic development, environmental protection, and international development. Moreover, Mr. Valdes has adopted a results-oriented approach to managing people and projects in diverse settings within the District of Columbia, Venezuela, and elsewhere. As the Chief Ward 1 Planner for the D.C. Office of Planning, he was instrumental in devising and disseminating the city's transit-oriented development guidelines, and successfully led a staff of urban planners, architects, and real estate development specialists to achieve neighborhood revitalization goals. During his tenure at the World Bank, Mr. Valdes managed a team of engineers, scientists, and technicians involved in devising, evaluating, and implementing technology transfer strategies to signatory counties of the Montreal Protocol. And while serving as a foundation representative with the Inter-American Foundation, Mr. Valdes pioneered a new approach to conducting international development in Latin America that involved forging ties with private-sector corporations as well as non-governmental organizations.

**Kelsey Walter** is Director of National Core Indicators-Aging and Disabilities (NCI-AD), of the National Association of States United for Aging and

Disabilities (NASUAD). Ms. Walter has worked as a Policy Associate at NASUAD since November 2012, and has been closely involved in the work to expand the NCI-AD since the beginning stages. In her new capacity, Ms. Walter will assist the NCI-AD Steering Committee as they finalize the adult consumer survey and support Georgia, Minnesota, and Ohio as they begin to pilot the new tool.

**Karen White, Ph.D.,** directs the Office of Statistical and Economic Analysis at Bureau of Transportation Statistics at the Department of Transportation. She has more than 26 years of experience as a Transportation Economist. Dr. White leads research measuring the role of transportation in the economy, transportation and economic cycles, performance management data, benefit–cost analysis, and the value of transportation to the economy.

Dr. White holds undergraduate degrees in Finance and Economics from The University of Texas at Austin and a Ph.D. in Economics from the University of Houston.

**Nigel Wilson, Ph.D.** came to the Massachusetts Institute of Technology in 1965 as a graduate student in transportation after completing his undergraduate degree at Imperial College in London. He studied with Professor Dan Roos and earned a Ph.D. in Civil Engineering with a transportation systems focus. He joined the faculty in 1970, the same year he graduated. He has since done research on urban transport systems for major cities around the world, including Boston, Chicago, San Juan, and now London, which was the second major city in the world (after Singapore) to successfully introduce congestion pricing. For most of the past 20 years, he has also run the interdepartmental M.S.T. program.

**Steve Yaffe** is the Transit Services Manager overseeing Arlington Transit (ART fixed route bus) and Specialized Transit for Arlington Residents (STAR) demand-responsive transit service. He is a former co-chair of the Mobility and Transportation Committee of the Fairfax Area Long-Term Care Coordinating Council & Disability Services Board. He also has served on the board of the ENDependence Center of Northern Virginia, a center for independent living. Prior to joining Arlington Transit, Mr. Yaffe was the planning manager for 16 years with FASTRAN, a human service transportation provider in Fairfax County, Virginia. He also has held transit and paratransit planning and oversight positions in Dayton, Ohio; Houston, Texas; and Sacramento, California. Mr. Yaffe is a former research coordinator and member of the Transportation Research Board's Paratransit Committee.

# E

# Structured Annotated Bibliography

Appendix E contains an annotated bibliography of the literature found at the intersection of health care and transportation. This is staff-prepared as background material relevant to the workshop topic and is included for informational purposes only.

Appendix E may be found at https://www.nap.edu/catalog/23638.